ARCHITECTURE OF INCARCERATION

ARCHITECTURE OF INCARCERATION

A.D. ACADEMY EDITIONS

ACKNOWLEDGEMENTS

Unless otherwise stated all illustrative material for the projects is courtesy of the architects.
Illustrative material was also kindly provided by Thomas A Markus; Leslie Fairweather;
The Architects' Journal, EMAP Architecture, London; United Nations Interregional Crime and
Justice Research Institute (UNICRI), Rome; Ron Haines, Director of Works at the Home
Office, Bob Pitcher and Ray Lawrence. Thank you to Petra Roth for her help with translation,
Dr Sean McConville for his input; and all the architects who responded with thoughts on
prison architecture, including Cedric Price, Ian Ritchie and Kisho Kurokawa.

Editorial Offices
42 Leinster Gardens London W2 3AN

EDITED BY IONA SPENS

House Editor: Maggie Toy
Art Editor: Andrea Bettella
Chief Designer: Mario Bettella
Designer: Laurence Scelles

Cover: Maison d'Arret de Brest, France (photograph: Deidi von Schaewen)
Page 2: Federal Correctional Institution, Marianna, Florida (photograph: Phil Eschbach)

First published in Great Britain in 1994 by
ACADEMY EDITIONS
An imprint of Academy Group Ltd
Member of the VCH Publishing Group

ISBN 1-85490-358-6

Distributed to the trade in the United States of America by
ST MARTIN'S PRESS
175 Fifth Avenue, New York, NY 10010

Printed and bound in Singapore

CONTENTS

Foreword

Judge Stephen Tumim, HM Chief Inspector of Prisons

Those of us with something of an appetite for prison architecture have had to satisfy ourselves to date with the splendid work of Robin Evans, The Fabrication of Virtue, English Prison Architecture 1750-1840, *which happily escapes and goes well beyond its dates. We have gorged on Michael Ignatieff's early book,* A Just Measure of Pain, The Penitentiary in the Industrial Revolution, 1750-1850. *We have trifled with Howard and Mayhew, and Janet Semple's Bentham; but only Evans is directly on the subject.*

Now comes an engaging savoury. Architecture of Incarceration *contains four professional essays and a wealth of photographs, showing mainly the new prisons of Europe and North America. Beyond almost every prison wall in the photographs, somewhat mysteriously emerges a blue sky, but perhaps that is intended to remind us of Oscar Wilde's prison recollection:*

> I never saw a man who looked
>
> With such a wistful eye
>
> Upon that little tent of blue
>
> Which prisoners call the sky,
>
> And at every drifting cloud that went
>
> With sails of silver by.

I remember tramping the beautiful hills above the sea at Montserrat in search of a site for a new prison. The Governor of that graceful island was determined that whatever prisoners were to get indoors, they should have a cheering prospect through the windows. There is no doubt, from my English experience, that good architecture and location encourage the regime of prisoners, and help both the prisoners and staff. I hope this book will stimulate both the architects and the clients of the architects.

Stephen Tumim

OPPOSITE: *HM Prison, Manchester (Strangeways), view through interior to original tower by Waterhouse (photograph: Chris Gascoigne)*

Introduction: 'A Simple Idea in Architecture'
Iona Spens

Throughout the world a variety of institutions and programmes exist for different offenders, including remand centres, low, medium and maximum security institutions and hospital facilities. Architecture is invested with an important outlet in providing 'correctional' facilities, as it moves apace with the pressure to house an increasing population of convicts, responding to legal systems and sentencing practices. Seminal is the currency of progressive thought about the purpose and nature of these buildings; now less discrete, this infusion has become pivotal to the design.

As we approach the millennium, appropriate measures of security need to be sought in an atmosphere that is humane and conducive to rehabilitation. Suitable programmes and activities are deemed necessary for the inmate's reintegration into society. The toughest prisons have not deterred crime: the problem will not be solved through correctional design. What is considered significant is that the inmate is not now impaired physically, emotionally or psychologically by his period of confinement.

The prison buildings which emerged in the late eighteenth and nineteenth century were designed in accordance with a philosophy that is now redundant. Stemming from the optimistic spirit of the Enlightenment and filtered through the ideas of such figures as Hanway, Beccaria, Eden, Howard and Bentham, separate or solitary confinement of the prisoner in his cell (not intended initially for long term convicts) was devised to effect punishment and prevent moral contamination, but also to act as a form of therapy, inducing reflection and repentance. The brief for the implementation of these systems was extensive, and even applied externally to the exercise yards. However, its most explicit translation can be seen in many prison chapel designs of this time, where the prisoner was to see and be seen by the chaplain, but the sides, backs, and fronts of the seats were to be 'made of such a height as to intercept communication between the seats'. Documenting the design of Perth Prison, the architect, in the First Report of Board of Director of Prisons in Scotland, 1840, wrote of a gallery to be formed around the base of the pulpit with seats for the officers of the prison 'from where they can see every prisoner in the chapel'.

The French philosopher Michel Foucault, effective in outlining fundamental changes in the nature of power relations since the late eighteenth century, emphasised a transition from punishment of the body to control of the mind or soul; manifested clearly in the panopticon (all-seeing) prison. Here, tiered cells were arranged in a centralised configuration, at the hub of which was positioned the guard's viewing tower. The design precept was to facilitate absolute observation with minimal staff supervision. Behind his protective shield of directional light, the guard could oversee the silhouetted prisoners who, unable to see their supervisor, felt under constant surveillance. Foucault's absorbing text on the theme, *Discipline and Punish: the Birth of the Prison* (1975), states that the major effect of the panopticon was to induce in the inmate 'a state of conscious and permanent visibility that assures the automatic functioning of power'; significantly, this power relation was independent of the person who exercised it. Jeremy Bentham was the architect preoccupied with developing the panopticon. Brother of its original devisor, Samuel, who was working in Russia, he envisioned that this institutional apparatus would have the following effect:

> Morals reformed, health preserved, industry invigorated, instruction diffused, public burthens lightened, economy seated as it were upon a rock, the gordian knot of the poor laws not cut but untied – all by a simple idea in architecture. ('Panopticon; or, the Inspection House' [1791], *Collected Works*, John Bowring, Vol IV, 1843)

The aim of this 'simple idea in architecture' was to strengthen social forces: the panopticon could be applied to any institution, including schools, hospitals and factories. Of interest, with a contemporary ring to our current situation, is that Bentham intended the panopticon, as both prison and factory, to be contracted out. Although he never saw his meticulously detailed contraption erected, it exerted a considerable influence on prison architecture and centralised planning and has been well analysed by Robin Evans, Michael Ignatieff and most recently by Janet Semple (see References and Select Bibliography, p128). Bentham's desire to inspire fellow philosophers beyond his time led him to arrange for his own body to be preserved as an auto-icon after his death.

The potency of the prison has been captured by many artists, including Piranesi in his spatially disconsonant *Carceri d'Invenzione* (c1750), and writers such as Oscar Wilde in *The Ballad of Reading Gaol* (1898). Jean Genet draws an interesting analogy between the prison and the palace in his provocative *The Thief's Journal* (1949):

> Prison offers the same sense of security to the convict as does a royal palace to a king's guest. They are the two buildings constructed with the most faith, those which give the greatest certainty of being what they are... The masonry, the materials, the proportions and the architecture are in harmony with a moral unity which makes these dwellings indestructible so long as the social form of which they are a symbol endures. The prison surrounds me with a perfect guarantee. I am sure that it was constructed for me – along with the law court, its annex, its monumental vestibule, designed for me in a spirit of the utmost seriousness.

Although at the other end of the spectrum, the majesty of the prison's appearance was often criticised. Reading Gaol, for example, was accused of resembling a ducal palace more than a place of incarceration. The architects of these large, imposing buildings drew on history for appropriate stylistic identity and character – just as Nazist ideology exploited the monumental forms of the neoclassical. A rich vocabulary of impregnable features was inaugurated; evident in the wealth of imposing, castellated prison buildings in existence today. Although the plan afforded the architect a certain degree of expressiveness – allowing him to use a variety of geometrical configurations to shape such large-scale commissions – the exterior was the most obvious outlet for the architect's creativity which was, naturally, quelled inside. Architects such as Sir John Soane and Robert Adam adopted the castellated theme to the context of prison design: their interpretations of this inspired functional tool, like those of others, are very much of their own time, marketed with embellishments for the gratification of a critical public.

That these structures were tailored extremely tightly to the prescriptions of the initial users continues to be brutally clear nowadays. Unable to meet changing standards in the penal system, original concepts are outmoded and the design brief of many prisons still in use is obsolete. Fortunately, stimulus for a coherent design approach can be found in extensively detailed guidelines, such as those set by the Federal Bureau of Prisons in the USA, the National Institute of Corrections' (NIC) *Small Jail Design Guide,* or the Home Office's *Prison Design Briefing System* (PDBS) in the UK.

Although the traditional prison and jail rhetoric is considered wholly inappropriate now in relation to the role and purpose of the current institution, it still pervades many recently executed exteriors, whether consciously or not. Encumbered by the necessary security ingredients of this architecture, it cannot be easy to convey an alternative guise. Contextual considerations are crucial, especially when this unpopular type is located in an urban site and subject to public criticism. Bartholomew County Jail (p58) in Columbus, a city

renowned for its architectural prowess, is one example of a building which despite its nature promotes an appropriate and attractive civic identity, responding to the existing context and character of the locale. Likewise, the massing, building height and material of Red Deer Remand Centre, Alberta (p80) allow the structure to blend with the adjacent courthouse. Visual buffering by existing vegetation or additional plantings also seems to be advocated in design guidelines for facilities situated near an urban location or road. Many new prisons reveal this increased attention to landscape considerations.

The correctional brief now directs more attention to the relationship between the staff and the inmate – deemed fundamental to the smooth functioning of the facility. Spatial organisation is instrumental in this respect. As is evident in the history of prisons, obsessively so in Bentham's case, unobstructed visual observation has been a persistent thread in the design of such buildings. However, gaining popularity is a view advocating that surveillance is not achieved by absolute visibility but by the officer's awareness of what is going on; inherent in many facilities adopting the direct supervision method of operation. As will be seen in this volume, this has driven a new breed of prison types, particularly in the United States, where the method is expounded in many publications, including those produced by the NIC. Other design and management categories commonly adopted there, where each state has its own system apart from the federal system, are the linear-intermittent surveillance method of operation and unit remote surveillance.

The attitude that it is politically safer to continue building traditionally is stoked by the belief that the inmates' behaviour will remain unaffected by a new correctional or managerial environment. In spite of this, it is interesting that the NIC, and subsequently other outfits such as the American Institute of Architects (AIA), the American Jails Association (AJA), and the American Correctional Association (ACA), had recognised the direct supervision method of

L TO R: *Jeremy Bentham, preserved and encased in the cloisters of University College, London (photograph courtesy of UCL). The old and the new: Holloway Women's Prison, London (photograph courtesy of the Home Office); HM Prison, Birmingham (photograph courtesy of Martin Charles); OVERLEAF: Cell door at Maison d'Arret, Brest*

operation by 1983. This method is in tune with the mode of thought which advocates that the contemporary institution should focus more on the effect of the environment on the individual, to correspond with our increased knowledge of human psychology. The institution is encouraged to be broken up into smaller, self-contained units, housing no more than forty to sixty inmates, comprised of cells arranged around a multi-use dayroom. In this 'open' space, within the boundary of a secure perimeter, the physical barriers are believed to be broken down as the officer interacts with the inmates.

An advantage of the direct supervision method concerns the role of the officer – it should not be forgotten that other users are subjected to the environment of these facilities, including visitors. Interaction with the inmates allows the officer in charge of his unit to adopt a more professional stance. Consequently, job satisfaction is inclined to be higher, resulting from the officer's progression from the monotony of his former duties where he was acting purely as a 'turn-key'. As to the fundamental question of cost – the major criticism of this building type – it is claimed that the provision of low-stress settings in direct supervision prisons and jails, incurs the same, and frequently less expenditure than indirect supervision models to design and operate. Secure furnishings and harder materials are commonly more expensive and invite vandalism.

The aim to foster a more positive environment is mediated by the creation of an environment that is proactive rather than reactive. An atmosphere devoid of hard furnishings, fixtures and other features associated with the rudimentary allocation of bodies in space, which anticipate vandalism or violence, is integral to this. Superseding the formally oppressive environment is a more open, communicative setting with less 'institutional' materials and fewer dehumanising features; widely pervaded by light and a more psychologically effective colour palette. This is believed to help reduce tension, and in the Frankfurt 'mother and child' facility shows an extremely sensitive approach to the interior (p90). Other prisons such as the ochre and blue 'Golden Sphinx' in Rotterdam (p108), design for Dordrecht Penitentiary (p110), or the arresting prison in Brest, reveal confident use of colour for more creative ends, whether exploited internally or externally. In certain examples, such as De Grittenborgh Penitentiary (p100) and the Maison d'Arret d'Epinal (p117), walls are also subject to interesting decorative treatment. Apparent throughout most of the new facilities is maximum exploitation of light, especially in dayroom areas, and, an increased concern for flexibility which is essential.

When the aesthetic boundaries are more relaxed for the architect – who is preferably integrated into the design process at an early stage – he can shape more adequately the physical and social environment to achieve positive behavioural expectations. Rendered with a wider range of architectural options, he is more likely to transcend the mere 'cosmetic' efforts of the past. According to Michael Walden of Dworsky Associates, one of the most difficult things for an architect to overcome is an apparent total lack of concern, or basic understanding on the part of an owner/client as to

a fundamental goal of the profession: the artistic endeavour to create spaces which can improve, enhance, and nurture the lives of all who come in contact with them. 'It is,' he states, 'only the agencies responsible for the construction of prisons and jails, one of the costliest building types to construct, that frequently indicate no desire to incorporate *architecture* into their facilities and in some cases actively discourage it. It has been our experience, in several recent designs, to have clients mandate that certain degrees of bleakness (one could argue ugliness) be incorporated'.

This aspect is wholly credible and particular to this architecture, which many architects do not wish to be associated with. It indicates the traditional muscle embedded in design and image, despite developments in penal thought. An unattractive building costs just as much as one designed with a view to aesthetic appeal. Whether one believes that the latter determines 'architecture', or that it is dependent on the outcome, what undoubtedly emerges from all this is not so much the question: 'are prisons architecture?' as: 'are prisons allowed to be architecture?' This precept is challenged by many projects in this volume; revealing a healthy form of pluralism.

More dignified accommodation in an environment which facilitates movement, interaction and change is evidently more conducive to rehabilitation and, ultimately, reintegration into society. Gaining popularity is the campus-like facility, with an assembly of parts that resembles an urban set-up; seen at centres in Fort Saskatchewan (p76) and Contra Costa (p46), for example.

With its many programmes, activities and human concentrate, the prison is a microcosm of a small town. A layout of this kind, though preferable with its spatial resonances and more human scale, requires adequate land. This is problematic when many new complexes are being sited in, or close to, urban locations for community interaction; the latter, coupled with physical control, also poses contradictory demands for the architect. If the convict population continues to escalate, alternative solutions must be sought – ideally, decent education, housing and health facilities would rehabilitate the offender before going to prison. In the meantime, research into the design of these institutions continues in various countries. In the Netherlands, for example, the focus applies to the development of a compact, low-rise prison (p92) that can be located in both a rural and urban context.

The sensorily impoverished space of the traditional prison layout with restricted control of movement clearly generates base behaviour and is counterproductive. In this volume, which is by no means a world-wide survey, a shortfall inevitably exists. However, what is hoped will be conveyed to the reader through the essays and projects is a sense of the history which gave form to the contemporary prison institution, the environment itself and some typical architectural interpretations and concepts in currency. As we 'progress' into the twenty-first century, perhaps the architect's role in shaping the prison vehicle will be more appropriate to the epoch, and the development of this type will correspond with those of other institutions. Prisons need to be more than human filing cabinets.

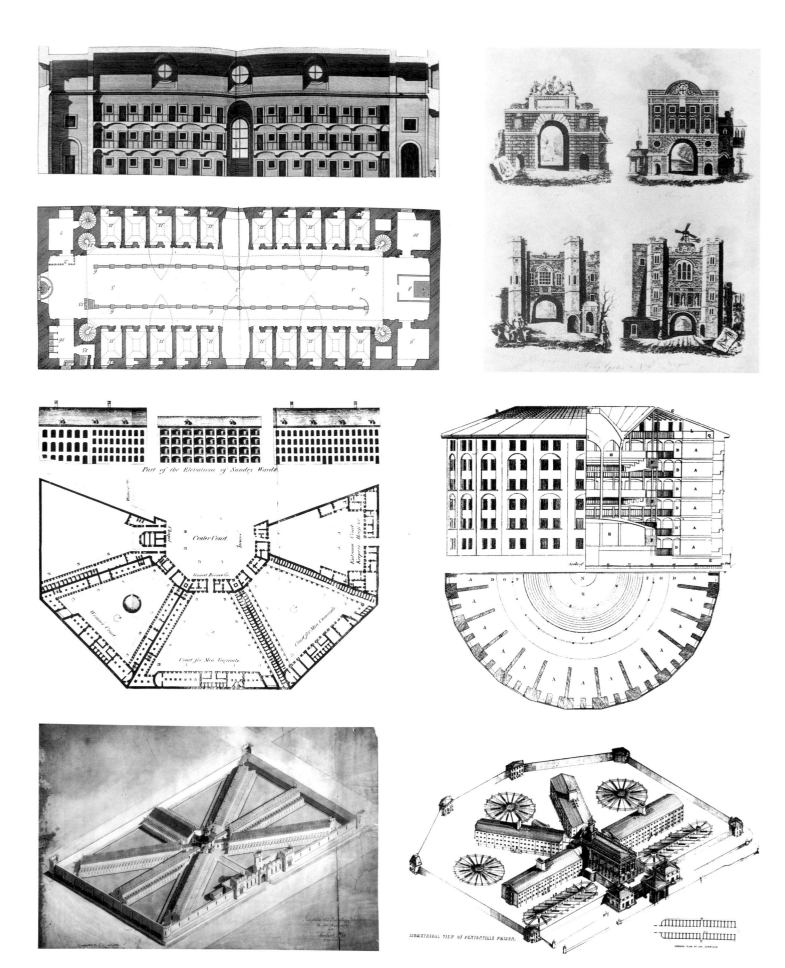

FROM ABOVE L TO R: *Young men's prison, San Michele, Rome (1701-04); London city gates, with Newgate on lower right; Maison de Force, Ghent (1772); Jeremy Bentham's Panopticon (1791), second version; Eastern State Penitentiary, Philadelphia (1821-29), aerial view (courtesy of BAL/RIBA); Pentonville Prison, aerial view*

Can History be a Guide to the Design of Prisons?

Thomas A Markus

T he history of the prison as a building type has been well researched in the last forty years. That work has shown how the random medieval carceral regimes reached a peak of size in the eighteenth century, when imprisonment was still unusual as a long term measure. It was used for extorting money from debtors, for felons awaiting trial or execution, and sometimes for torture to extract confessions. Petty criminals, vagrants and prostitutes were often confined to a period of enforced labour, a system that was greatly expanded in post-Elizabethan 'Bridewells'. The carceral space was often mixed up with space for the physically or mentally ill, the old and infirm, and even orphanages, in a variety of 'hospitals', poorhouses and workhouses. Functional and spatial categories were imprecise. When imprisonment was the only or main function, the buildings were often located at the edges of towns – within the walls or, more usually, incorporated into town gates. Six of London's eight original City gates contained prisons; the most famous, Newgate giving its name to London's chief eighteenth-century gaol.

If we examine this locational strategy more closely, something which is still important today becomes evident. From ancient times the walls around the edges of towns marked the boundary between human, artificial creation and the natural world of the gods. Foundation ceremonies in Classical times included the ploughing of a furrow along the line on which the town walls would be built, with the plough lifted at the place where the four gates would occur, thus leaving an undisturbed strip of earth between the two worlds. Jumping over the sacred furrow was, as indeed later climbing over the wall would be, a capital offence. On completion of this task the team of oxen would be offered in a ritual sacrifice at the place where the forum would be built, to propitiate the gods who might be angered by this daring behaviour which imitated their own creativity. The gate was liminal, a threshold place; a dangerous no man's land where social and spatial categories broke down. To guard against the category ambiguities of a threshold, elaborate ritual surrounded entry through the gate and, architecturally too, this element became heavily ornamented and elaborated.

If a town or building is regarded as a metaphoric body one can see in all this reflections of the taboos and rituals which, as Mary Douglas shows, surround the orifices of the human body. These are for the passage of food, waste elimination or sexual intercourse, and are liminal; breaking down in this case the clear categories of what is self and what is not. Not surprisingly then, if a town wall is seen as a barrier against the intrusion of impurity or foreign elements, places such as hospitals and cemeteries are located outside. This is not only a sensible practical precaution but is because these places are metaphors for contamination. A prison, therefore, is located outside or at the boundary where its impurity – in this case of a moral kind – can be made visible and filtered out before it contaminates the interior insidiously.

It was on the same principle that Ledoux, in laying out his production Utopia of Chaux in the 1770s, placed the entry gate between the house of the guards and the prison. One can see precisely the same symbolic drive for purity in the transportation of convicts to remote colonies, enclosing them in floating hulks on river estuaries, and putting prisons on remote moors.

The settlement boundaries in relation to which prisons were located were clearly marked, and penetrated only by a few, carefully controlled apertures. However, up to the eighteenth century the boundary of the prison itself was quite the opposite: loosely defined and penetrated in many ways. Goods, persons, information and people passed freely in and out, controlled only by the keeper for his profit. Prisons had taprooms, stalls, shops and barbers, and often the keeper would run the female section as a brothel, with clients introduced by means of various transitional spaces and activities. Within this permeable boundary there were certainly distinctions by economic class: those with money had more and better quality space, their own servants and good food whilst the poor prisoners had to rely to an extent on charitable donations of food, goods or money, often handed over through grated begging windows. But categories other than those based on personal wealth and its concomitant social status were mixed up in a society of chaos, squalor and disease (which recognised no class boundaries).

It was the Enlightenment which brought reason and order into this state of affairs. Outstandingly influential were the theories of Beccaria (1764) which emphasised the need for proportionality between a crime and its punishment, discipline and orderly productive labour, and Howard's writings (in the last quarter of the eighteenth century) based on a vast programme of visits, with their emphases on classification of prisoners, segregation of categories, ventilation, hygiene, useful labour and religious services. The classification he proposed was based on gender, age and type of crime. He designed some model prisons on these lines and his writings, illustrated with fine engravings, gave wide publicity to some major European prisons. Among these were the 1770s Maison de Force at Ghent with its central octagonal court, around which were arranged eight trapezium-shaped courts for different categories of prisoners; and the Papal prison for young men, San Michele in Rome, which in view of its date (1701-04) was 'prophetic'. Here the cells were ranged on either side of an open central hall, opening off open galleries on the upper two floors. The main hall was used for wool spinning, carried out in silence (hence the popular name for the prison: 'the Silentium') under close surveillance. Each cell had individual sanitation and its internal apertures angled so that the central altar at one end of the open hall was visible.

The principle of central altars, chapels and churches in hospital and other institutional buildings, often designed so that inmates could participate as spectators in religious services, was strongly established; an early design for such a scheme was Filarete's fifteenth-century ideal hospital for Sforzinda. Underlying this tradition was the unity of inmates whether physically, mentally or morally sick, within an all-encompassing scheme of divine providence. Howard referred to this as a 'Catholic' tradition.

Though it was certainly more explicit in France, Italy and Spain, even in his own and other British schemes the prison chapel came to occupy a central, axial position; often a symbolic rather than a practical proposition, for actual visibility of the altar was rarely achieved. The principle was that this geometric centre drew the gaze of all towards itself, in return for which, metaphorically, God saw and encompassed all. Under the powerful influence of Bentham's Panopticon (1791), the metaphor and the practice was turned inside out in what Gertrude Himmelfarb has called a haunted house. At the centre was now located the Governor or Inspector. He kept all under continuous surveillance but, by careful control over geometry and lighting, was invisible to all. The inmates, instead of gaining a solidarity by being drawn centripetally to a symbolic centre, were fragmented and dispersed centrifugally from the centre by a powerful and invisible eye.

Enlightenment rationality, the political upheavals of the French Revolution and the social upheavals of the industrial revolution – massive urbanisation, a mobile and often unemployed population, public disorder, squalor and disease – created a reaction of control and discipline. The prison was but the clearest case of the general shift, based on fear, towards rational and rigid order.

The enormous nineteenth-century elaboration of theories and practices in prison discipline and management were, in microcosm, theories and practices of social order. The two most powerful, and competing penal regimes were the silent and the separate systems. The former, often named the 'Auburn' after the New York prison where it was first developed at the beginning of the nineteenth century, allowed prisoners to mix for work, religious services and exercise; but by management rules of a punitive kind, rather than rules built into the space itself, imposed a strict regime of silence. It was thought that this non-communication would be an effective way of preventing the spread of moral contagion. The latter used space as a way of isolating and separating each prisoner so that, as far as possible, he or she neither saw nor heard another. The most famous early prison to implement this idea was Philadelphia's Eastern State Penitentiary (1821-29) designed by the British architect Haviland. Each of the seven arms of the radial plan, initially for a total 250 prisoners on a single ground floor had a central passage, on either side of which lay the cells with private gardens – not unlike the traditional plan for a Carthusian monastery. The word 'penitentiary' itself signified the same religious idea of penitence in silent solitude.

On the whole the American institutions followed the silent model, whereas in Britain and Continental Europe a stronger moral line led to the adoption of the separate model.

The largest and best known British example was Pentonville (1840-42), with four, three-storey halls of cells radiating from the central chapel. These halls bore an uncanny resemblance to the Papal Silentium built almost 140 years earlier. The individual cells had full sanitation and provided hand-turned cranks with attached counters, where prisoners could be forced to perform a set number of turns each day. The tread wheel, whose sails could be adjusted to offer more or less air resistance, thus adjusting the effort required to the severity of punishment considered appropriate, and the masks and hoods prisoners wore when they moved into the chapel to sit in individual, isolated cubicles, all combined to enforce the underlying principle of individual reform through penitence and labour, which would rehabilitate the prisoner.

By 1847 some 51 prisons of this kind had been erected or were under construction in Britain alone. It was well into the second half of the century before the full horrors of the system caused it to be diluted and ultimately discredited and abandoned.

Of course its remnants survive, mainly in the buildings themselves which, with two or three prisoners in each cell, and, until very recently, the abandonment of individual sanitation for 'slopping out', provide the worst of the old and the new worlds. There is neither privacy, nor the possibility of social relations being established on the basis of choice. In its place enforced relations, with all the attendant problems of drugs, enforced sexual activity, and mutual 'learning' of criminal behaviour, in many ways have recreated the problems which Howard attacked over two centuries ago.

Space

The plan, and the symbolic and ideological forms with which these buildings were invested, are certainly of interest and have a vital role in explaining the internal power relations of the regimes. They also make important statements about external social relations concerning how the prison is to be seen by society as an instrument of social policy. But such features are evident 'surface' phenomena. A deeper feature, which is not immediately evident, is their spatial structure.

The study of this is a relatively new field innovated by Professor Hillier and his colleagues at University College London.

It deals with how the spaces are organised with respect to each other and the outside world in terms of 'nextness' – what other spaces is each space next to and penetrable from. This is a question of topology, not geometry. If all the interconnections are marked on a plan and then plotted on a 'graph' so that the first space (say an entrance hall) one encounters is at level one, all those one can then move on to at level two, and so on, a characteristic network appears. Two of its features are depth, and the degree to which it contains rings or trees. Depth refers to the total number of levels to reach one space from another – say from the outside to the innermost. A ring indicates that one can move from a space through others and return to one's starting point by a different route; whereas in a tree one has no choice but to move backwards and forwards along the branches and the trunk. Both properties have been shown to relate to social interactions, encounters, surveillance and control, in other words to the social relations in the building. It is not that they 'reflect' these relations; they actually embed them in a material form. Society is never a-spatial nor is space ever a-social.

Now Hillier et al argue that buildings control relations by controlling the interfaces between three categories of people: 'strangers', 'visitors' and 'inhabitants'. Strangers are the general mass of people who have no normal reason to come into a building. One purpose of buildings is to keep them out. Visitors are those strangers who temporarily have a reason to enter. In many cases the building's *raison d'être* is to bring them in. They may be visitors to a museum, customers in a shop, audiences in a theatre or drinkers in a pub. Inhabitants own or control the building and have power invested in it. In the instances given they would be the director and museum staff, the shopkeeper, the company director, actors and production staff, and the pub landlord. Visitors are kept to relatively shallow, often ringy, outer spaces, and inhabitants occupy the deeper, often tree-like ones; the deepest space often signifying that its occupant wields the maximum power. The interface between them occurs in such places as the museum gallery, the shop counter, the proscenium arch and the pub bar.

According to these theories there is one type of building where this structure is inverted; visitors are in the deepest spaces, and increasing depth signifies decreasing power, whilst inhabitants occupy the outer, shallow zones. The former are often at the tips of branches of a tree-like structure, the latter are in ringy space with freedom of choice. This is the spatial definition of an institution such as a prison, hospital asylum, workhouse, school or, to a lesser degree, factory. Here visitors (whose 'visit' may have a duration of years) are denied unsupervised direct communication because this is impossible across the tips of the branches of a tree, without going through the common root, which also lies on an inhabitant ring and is thus controlled. In other words, the conditions for obtaining communal power through solidarity are denied.

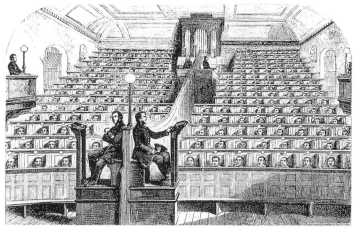

FROM ABOVE: *Hand-turned crank in a 'separate' cell; male and female hooded convicts; Pentonville Prison, chapel interior*

Often a plan seems to deny this inversion. For instance Robert Adam's fourth design for the 1791 Edinburgh Bridewell, heavily influenced by Jeremy Bentham except that the circular Panopticon has become a half circle, had two crucial spaces from which its inhabitants could control the regime by surveillance. One was the central inspection tower, from which all the cells were visible. The other was a small exterior inspection tower from which all the exercise yards, separated by walls to keep categories of prisoners apart, were under surveillance. This second tower appears to be deep inside the plan – not the location where inhabitants should be in such a building. However it is connected to the internal inspection tower by a basement corridor. This simple device brings the second tower right to the surface, shallow spatial zone, only one step deeper than the internal tower. Indeed tunnels and bridges always have this function – to leapfrog over metric space and bring into adjacency spaces which might otherwise be many steps apart or might even be impossible to connect on the same plane due to the co-presence of other, adjacent intermediate spaces.

Design goal

In studying these prisons of the last two centuries one can see all of today's goals of imprisonment, often dimly articulated and confused. They can be summarised under five headings.

PUNISHMENT: Here the prison is seen as a deterrent, both to re-offending by its inmates and to offending by those outside. The harshness of the regime is intended to 'cure' the former of, and frighten the latter from, criminal behaviour. The infliction of necessary suffering is also seen, though rarely acknowledged, as a way for society to seek retribution. Buildings therefore need to reinforce the control, surveillance, discomfort, alienation and loss of privacy which such a regime requires.

PROTECTION: If prisoners are considered dangerous, threatening life, property or ideology, the main requirement of both regimes and buildings is to create a fully controlled and secure boundary along the social and physical perimeter. What happens within the boundary can then be determined by other goals. Clearly, the building or its site requires strong physical boundaries, and it might be located in a remote location so as to make both escape and the participation of outside conspirators more difficult. There might also be the requirement for some secure internal boundaries, to prevent the more dangerous inmates from attacking those who are less so.

REFORM: Here the emphasis is on the acquisitions of moral, social or religious habits of thought and attitudes as a basis for behaviour. Solitary confinement, education, religious practices, social training, labour, disciplined and regulated communal life have all, at various times, been seen as serving this goal. The building then requires quite specific spaces and spatial organisation for these activities and the controlled interaction of prisoners with each other and with the staff.

CURE: This is the medical model, where criminal behaviour is seen as more of a personal than a social pathology, which therapy may cure or at least alleviate. Despite the massive evidence of the close connection between, on the one hand, early social deprivation, personality disorders, psychological illness and mental handicap of various degrees of severity, and criminal behaviour on the other, few modern prisons are designed or run as therapeutic institutions. Clearly the chief requirement would be adequate resources for skilled staff. But there would be spatial implications too. For instance any group therapy or activities designed to foster the acquisition of social responsibility and skill, require spaces for appropriate sizes of groups, and also spaces where the institution's inmates and those outside – family, friends and community workers – can mix in an environment which allows both privacy and social interaction.

EXEMPLARY RIGHTEOUSNESS: The prison can be a public statement of moral, political and social virtue. It then becomes primarily a symbolic, allegorical or metaphoric object, where the internal life of its inmates is less important than the message which is transmitted to society. In that perspective the building, as a static monument, is far more important than the regime. And especially its formal imagery becomes important. Such imagery has included the military, the baronial, the noble 'Classical', the 'homely' Tudor or medieval, the small scale 'cottage', and the vernacular.

There are some who deny that the prison has any validity or usefulness as a social institution of the future, and, unless they take up the position of nihilism, they have to develop alternative ideas, practices and institutions to cope with criminal behaviour. For those who hold this position, a critique of current regimes and their buildings is irrelevant. However for those who see some future in prisons, even though they may propose quite radically new systems, any vision must include ideas about both buildings and regimes. And one way of imagining alternatives is to analyse past and present models based on various amalgams of the five goals of incarceration outlined above and subject them to a critique based on social relations. Out of that critique possible alternatives emerge.

Social relations

The reason for starting with social relations is because criminal behaviour is the visible outcome of personal or social pathological relations. One way of defining the goal of imprisonment is in terms of change in these relations. For several reasons such a definition will encompass relations outside the prison too. First, because prisoners form part of an existing network with relatives and friends, which, to a greater or lesser degree will survive or even develop. Secondly, because staff and other workers in the prison have their own relations outside. And thirdly, because the narrative web whose endpoint is someone's imprisonment is known to entail early childhood, education, social agencies, housing, health, employment and economic circumstances – the

RIGHT TO BELOW LEFT: *Robert Adam's Edinburgh Bridewell (1791), exterior view; spatial maps of a 'pure tree' prison; 'diluted tree' prison; 'closed net' prison; 'open net' prison; the 'hamlet' (refer to 'Making Relations Concrete' overleaf).*

THE PURE TREE: *This plan resembles the traditional nineteenth-century prison, and represents the inverted type in its undiluted form. Entrance is through a secure 'gate', a series of outer courts, control buildings and inhabitant spaces. Three of these (B, C and D) lie on the only ring in the building. In this example cells and communal buildings are entered from a cloister-like internal space (D) one of which (G) leads to a deeper space (H) which in turn leads to a communal day hall (I), that will have prison staff on duty when it is in use. It is from here that the cells (J-T) open. They are on the tips of branches at the deepest point of the spatial structure. Communication between them is not possible directly, but only through the root of the branches (I) – a space shared by prisoners and staff and hence always under surveillance. There would be no possibility of freely chosen friendships being developed in a private space. The fact that both visitors and inhabitants share a single entrance sequence implies both a degree of solidarity between them – they are both cut off from the outside world in exactly the same way – but also a very strict regime of surveillance and control. The overall depth, at seven layers, is great.*

THE DILUTED TREE: *This has the same spaces and formal features as the previous design. The only change is that there is extra secure 'gate' from the outside, and some of the communal spaces are directly interconnected, making communication possible without entering the 'cloister'. The result is a structure with a number of rings; some of which, for example, D-I-H, allow some freedom for choosing encounter-generating and encounter-avoiding routes. In this structure prisoners may identify one gate as being their own and also belonging to their visiting friends and relatives, and the other as belonging to staff and official visitors. As a result of these changes the overall depth, at three, is much less.*

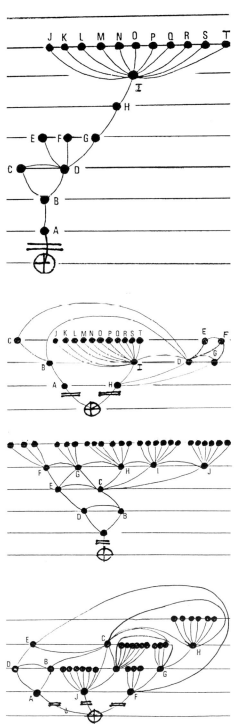

THE CLOSED NET: *Here again there is a single point of controlled entry. But internally the space is now fragmented into separate clusters, in each of which is a group of cells and associated shared communal space. These form clustered branches in the depth of the structure. Some group identity will exist and variation in group size. Spaces, such as C, connect to each subgroup and integrate the entire prison. Moreover, the connections are rich and result in a complex system of rings. The overall depth, at four layers, lies between the first and second examples.*

THE OPEN NET: *Like the previous design, this has a shallow, ringy structure, but with several 'gates' through the secure boundary. Two of these – but it could be any number – lead straight into one of the communal spaces which connect a small cluster of cells. In other words, each unit now has its own entrance. There is still a 'main' gate for the inhabitants' use. Many possible routes exist between units. This might be the characteristic layout of a prison whose inmates go out to work, make visits to their homes, have weekend or longer paroles, receive conjugal visits, and participate in the local community's sports, cultural or social events. The association of an entrance with each cluster gives each of these much identity and independence.*

THE HAMLET: *This title has been chosen to represent the idea of small, relatively isolated units in which prisoners and staff can form communities with a high degree of internal cohesion. The links between units are relatively sparse and, if need be, highly controlled. Each unit, as well as the central prison facilities and administration, has its own link to the outside. The resulting spatial structure is shallow and relatively ringy. But the trees constituted by the cell groups of each unit are clearly evident, as is the much greater ringyness of the central block.*

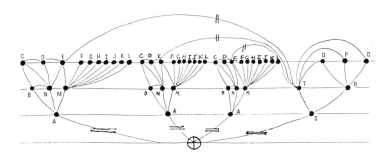

entire social fabric. In other words any critique of the prison today is a critique of society. And any prescription for the prison of tomorrow is a prescription for tomorrow's society. If prisoners are to come to terms with themselves, with society and with some larger scheme of things, what model of 'normal' social relations is available? Here there is a severe problem: the 'normal' has always consisted of asymmetrical power relations. This is not a phenomenon of today. The manifestations of class divisions and conflict vary throughout history, with some features remaining constant: huge gaps between rich and poor, deprived and privileged; differences in access to the law, education and political power; inequalities of access arising from differences in gender, class, race, age and physical and mental power; and reliance on armed force, domestically and internationally, as the ultimate sanction.

Some manifestations are more specific to today: the globalisation of capital extending these asymmetries and conflicts internationally; access to, and the power of the media; personal and institutional competition, with market forces as engine for change; urban ghettos of deprivation and enormous squatter settlements; macho and even violent advertising; and ecological exploitation. Such a picture of power relations may be a bleak model, but it is real. Of course the critique of power is justice, and, both outside and inside the prison, establishing the rule of justice is an obvious goal. But no less real, though less visible, are counter forces, almost 'subversive' relations, which are omnipresent alongside the power relations and are able to heal pathologies: solidarities of all kinds; community-based enterprises; 'green' politics; the strength of family and friendship bonds; critical literature and teaching; creative, artistic activity.

If the 'normal' social relations of which the prison may become a microcosmic model are of justice and healing bonds, a paradox is immediately evident. Without denying individual freedom and responsibility, it is nevertheless clear that here is an institution which mops up those who are most severely affected by social pathologies to which, as an institution, it may itself be a contributor. Yet, even assuming it could be based on an alternative social model, its inmates, possibly the most vulnerable members of society, when they emerge will once again be in a society which to a degree is pathological. To enable them to carry over a countervailing set of relations is to demand of those who may be most damaged a degree of heroism which even the most able to cope might find too much. The result is that once again, but for different reasons, the ex-prisoners would be alienated misfits and loners. The more successful the prison, the more true this would be.

There seem to be several answers. First, the prison, in microcosm, has to be a visible cell of good living, a demonstration of just power relations and rich bonds, but within the discipline which incarceration implies. What a tall order! This will set targets for the internal relations within the community of prisoners, within the community of staff and other workers, between the two communities, and between both groups and external structures. Secondly, the regime must identify, both at a general level and for each individual prisoner, those external structures of this kind which will serve as 'hooks' onto which he or she can fasten. This implies a process of building on these connections from the very start of the period of imprisonment. And thirdly, whatever therapy, education or development is undertaken by and for individuals, the goal must always be the enrichment of present and future social relations, as indeed it should be in society outside.

Making relations concrete

Bearing in mind these comments, and the five historic goals of imprisonment, it is useful to examine the meanings of, and prescriptions for, a few archetypal designs from the point of view of space (see page 17). Underlying each is the principle of a secure boundary whose penetrations are controlled by 'gates'. Therefore the variations in social relations which the plans imply are limited to internal movement and surveillance, the way staff and prisoners' spaces relate, and the degree of identification of sub-units and their links with the outside.

In each of these regimes order is created by establishing a degree of hierarchy – not only between visitors and inhabitants, but within the inhabitant community – cells, groups of cells with shared facilities, units, and the whole prison. Since the organisation then takes on the form of a tree, tall or flat, not unnaturally so does the space. Such organisations are rigid, predictable and work by control of all interactions at each level as well as between levels. They leave little room for chance events or encounters, choice, crossing of hierarchical thresholds, or change. Therefore the idea of individual change or development, which cannot be programmed or predicted, is a contradiction within such a structure, despite the fact that the rhetoric might well be that it is just such individual change which is the chief goal.

Of course, an infinite number of possible variations can be built around these archetypes; the hamlet could be physically disjointed into independent units with links established by electronic means and controlled internal transport. On the other hand, if the regime lies at the extreme 'open end' of the 'open'-'closed' dimension, prisoners may be free to move between the units, and their own unit and the outside, with minimum surveillance. A key variable is the presence of work as a part of the regime. The type of work, the required training and skills, the method of production, whether entirely carried out inside the prison or by some linkage with a production enterprise outside – all these will have spatial consequences. What is clear, however, is that as long as secure boundaries with controlled 'gates' are maintained, the type of variation is limited.

More radical alternative regimes would demand equivalent departures in spatial structure. One can speculate on a few; for instance, if relatively independent units were to be located in densely built-up urban areas, the connections with outside resources like shops, libraries, colleges, sports, recreational facilities and housing would become complex and the strategies for 'gate' control by staff, or internal monitoring by prisoners themselves, would also be complex. On the other hand, a prison on a remote rural site, in which most resources have to be provided internally, would require fewer (hence more easily controlled) 'gates'.

Location

The selection of a prison site is as complex an issue as the design of the prison itself. Land costs, security, attitudes of the local community, housing for staff, travel distance for prisoners' relatives and friends, and availability of community resources will all enter into the equation. And all will have specific design consequences. Two traditions have become established over time; both have already been mentioned. One is that of locating prisons at the boundaries of, or outside urban settlements, as a way of maintaining 'civic purity'. The other is that of removing prisoners to a location as far away as possible. Hence galley slaves, transportation to colonies, floating hulks, and remote moorland sites have been used. Of course all these are in conflict with any policy which aims to maintain existing and build new social relations for prisoners.

Metaphoric image

The location of prisons in town walls or gates not only achieved the purifying objectives already discussed, but resulted in rugged, castle-like materials and forms. These stylistic images were continued into the eighteenth and nineteenth centuries. Heavy rustication, portcullissed gates, small and barred windows, (sometimes reduced to slits), battlements, towers and solid peripheral walls became standard, and were adapted to any style: Classical, Gothic, Scottish Baronial or eclectic. The Neo-classical French architects of the late eighteenth century went further in developing allegorical or metaphoric forms in line with the theory of architecture parlance. Prison design became a favourite example for these theories. Boullée for instance describes his design for a severe, Classical courthouse ('Palace of Justice') sitting on top of a solid podium in which was located the prison: 'It seemed to me that in presenting this august palace raised on the shadowy lair of Crime, I should not only show to advantage the nobility of the architecture on account of the resulting contrasts, but I should also have an impressive metaphorical image of Vice overwhelmed by the weight of Justice'. According to his contemporary, Ledoux, designer of the prison and courthouse at Aix: 'The temple illuminated by justice forms a salutary opposition to the dark places devoted to crime.' The famous French prison of La Roquette uses precisely these forms and images, as indeed, do hundreds of other European and American cases.

Metaphoric forms are powerful. But they can be used not only to reinforce the meaning of prisons but as camouflage. To some extent recent architectural developments might be seen as camouflage. In the name of creating a 'community', the vast institutions have become fragmented into smaller, low units, in which vernacular materials such as brick and timber, sloping roofs, dormers and picturesque cottage gardens feature. What, often, is not evident is that the spatial structure, functional programme and institutional regime which accompany these forms often bear much greater similarity to their nineteenth-century precursors than do their novel forms. In the end, those are likely to influence the quality of life and social relations in a much more powerful, and lasting way, than the formal imagery.

The fabrication of virtue

This is the title of the late Robin Evans' scholarly book on the history of the nineteenth-century English prison. He interprets its architecture not as something which reflects the institution but as a vital instrument in carrying out its goals. It embodies, in a material way, the abstract ideological and social theories which are beneath any prison regime. Because the prison may undergo evolutionary, or even quite radical, revolutionary, change, this will not cease to be the case. Obviously straightforward functional demands for security, durability, sanitation, communications, energy, maintenance and adaptability have to be met. Modern means of surveillance and communication may change the way some of this is done, but do not remove the potency of buildings, because people have material bodies. Whatever their patterns of organisation and relations, these bodies are always located some*where* in space. The structure of that space, and the metaphoric images of the enclosing elements which articulate it, will remain as key materialisations of penal social theory; its practice. We had better get them right.

Boullée's Palace of Justice (1780s)

The Landlocked Fleet

Peter Wayne

Leonardo da Vinci was convinced that working in a small room helped to concentrate his energies into the task at hand. The smaller the cubic capacity of the workplace, the less chance of ephemeral distractions, the purer the thought process. In the nature of things, and having myself inhabited (for 11 years) an average of four different cells in 30 different prisons throughout the United Kingdom, I think I can lay some claim to authority on the subject. I write this piece from a cell. Let the resulting text be the counterbalance against which the reader may weigh the authenticity of Leonardo's hypothesis.

What is the philosophy behind what has collectively become known as the architecture of incarceration? What linking strands can we draw across a canvas of eclectic architectural hotchpotch stretching from Peterhead Prison perched high on precipitous cliffs on the north-east coast of Scotland, to dour dank Dartmoor, immutably cold and grey on the edge of our most fearsome national park?

Sir Richard Rogers told me recently that when he designed his controversial Lloyds Building in the City of London, he deferred to the vast brick and cast iron atria prevalent in so many of our Victorian prisons. 'Functionalism,' he stated categorically. 'Both Norman Foster and I adhere to the functional aspects of penal architecture and try to use them in the High Tech process.'

This functionalism, which harks back to Louis H Sullivan's 'rule that shall permit of no exception' to wit that 'form follows function', is the one element ubiquitous in the shaping of over two hundred penal institutions in Britain today. Be it a borstal, detention centre, remand centre, long term, short term, open, closed, local allocation, or so called 'dispersal' prison, fabric and form almost always (there are some notable exceptions which will be discussed later in this essay) ignore any aesthetic consideration – surely a *sine qua non* of any challenging architectural brief – which one might normally expect in commissions of such monumental proportions.

I would like to address myself to the psychological effect of such manifestations in the enclosure of space upon the individual therein imprisoned. To do this, I will define three major and very broad classifications of building within the penal microcosm.

Firstly, we should consider the Victorian radial prisons; let us call them the aircraft carriers of this landlocked fleet. Built in some cases by the prisoners themselves, the very names of these town and city prisons are enough to evoke awe and fear into the mind of any citizen rash enough to contemplate a descent into the *demi-monde* of criminality. HM prisons Wandsworth and Pentonville in London, Strangeways in Manchester, Armley in Leeds, Winson Green in Birmingham, Oxford, Reading, Exeter and Durham are but a few examples of these outdated but living relics of another age.

The Victorians were most adept at architectural onomatopoeia. Their prisons looked authoritarian from without and within. Today, as a prisoner passes through their ominous gatehouses (Wandsworth's original was loosely copied from Vanbrugh's Seaton Delaval) he is confronted with all manner of intimidating features and unexpected eccentricities, many now listed as historical monuments. Venetian campaniles, Roman entablatures, soaring Gothic watertowers, neo-Byzantine chapels, amphitheatres, classical rotundas, Soanian windows, eerie barrel-vaulted underground cellars . . . The mood is set from the very beginning. Behave, beware and buckle under. As the gangplanks are now drawn in, the prisoner weakens and obeys.

Packed to overflowing capacity in the late twentieth century, radial prisons offer cellular accommodation of the most basic kind; arranged in rows, one locked door after another, rising on top of each other to two, three, or four storeys, on wings radiating like the spokes of a cartwheel from the central rotunda.

On each level, galleries or landings no more than a yard wide run around the entire building, joining at the centre end of each wing, before leading off again along adjacent halls. Prior to the recent installation of thick steel bars and gates at the entrance to each self-contained wing, it was possible to walk around these galleries without interruption throughout the whole prison. Up one wing, along its back width, back down to the centre, up, along and down its neighbour and so on *ad infinitum* until one grew bored of the exercise, dropped of exhaustion, or was spotted by an eagle-eyed warden on the centre (from where, significantly, it is possible to observe every wing simply by turning 360 degrees) and returned forthwith to one's cell.

The whole is an enormous enclosure of space, top-lit from secular clerestories, and, at the far end of the halls, by gargantuan round-headed windows rising atria-like from floor to ceiling, not dissimilar to, but on a far more monumental scale, than those in so many of our atmospheric baroque churches in the City of London. Great shafts of yellow and white light sometimes penetrate the thick, opaque glass. One feels like some rare exotic bird, trapped in an intricate gilded cage; a metaphor not inappropriate as the hammer beamed roofs frequently resound to the flapping of real birds, curious and unfortunate enough to have found their way into these vast basilicas of human discontent.

It is once inside the cell that the prisoner really begins to feel the oppressiveness of these city fortresses. There are some small dimensional differences between cells in the various prisons, but more often than not, living space for 23 hours a day, seven days a week, averages 800 cubic feet; that is 8 × 13 × 9. Roofs are shallow arches, so it is easy to imagine oneself on the Orient or Trans-Siberian Express taking some never ending journey to the edge of the world. These cells look like gutted sections of railway carriages without the panoramic windows. The only window in evidence here is sunken into the back wall, too high to look out of, and usually double-barred. Standing underneath this aperture, one glances up at Oscar Wilde's 'little tent of blue the prisoners call sky'. They say that thick walls provide the best protection against nuclear attack. It is one of the screws' stock in trade funny lines when you protest about claustrophobia. But overcrowding means that two, sometimes three prisoners live in this environment. Is it any wonder that the moulded chamber pots permanently carry a thick urinary crust and nearly knock one out with the stench of ammonia the minute the lid is lifted?

What are the psychological effects of having to defecate in front of two other people, on a piece of newspaper laid out on the floor? Imagine if one of your cellmates is a schizophrenic (no statistics are available to the present writer, but reliable sources estimate that up to a third of the prison population suffers from varying degrees of schizophrenia) – it seems that prolonged lengths of sensory deprivation blur the imagination with reality and the sufferer wakes up in the middle of the night chatting loudly to Sir Walter Raleigh, or fighting off an imaginary attack from a swarm of wasps. One learns patience and disregards modesty. A human being adapts – or goes under.

There are of course lighter, even tender moments. I once found myself locked up for nearly a year with a Romany gypsy. He was completely illiterate, and I felt for him. To suffer these conditions with the escape hatch that literature provides is quite unbearable enough. Shane couldn't read a word. He would stare blankly into space for hour after hour, day after day. Eventually, because it was driving me mad as well, I suggested I might read a book out aloud to him, and reluctantly, he agreed. I chose for this cellular 'Book at Bedtime', Charles Dickens' *Oliver Twist*, which in the end took over two weeks to get through. One night, with the 60-watt lightbulb lending a particularly crepuscular air to the proceedings, I was reading the passage where, after Oliver has been taken to the safety of the countryside by his guardians, Fagin's face appears at the window of the boy's bedroom. It is the middle of the night and a fierce storm is raging outside. I got to the moment when Oliver, only bordering on the conscious, opens his eyes and recognises the old Jew's face. Fear jumps off the page. Shane and I experienced at exactly the same moment, the feeling that somebody, somewhere, had just walked over our graves. He stopped and whispered, 'Read that passage again Peter. It was realer than the real thing'. I read it again more slowly

FROM ABOVE: *Interior of the Lloyds Building (photograph: Janet Gill); typical Victorian prison interior, c1850, frequented by members of the public*

and the effect on both of us was just as powerful and unnerving. We had reached a moment of absolute communication, but it took hours to get to sleep that night.

My second broad category of building type, the spurred prison, came into being after the Mountbatten Commission's review of the penal system in the mid-sixties. It was decided than that the Victorians' vision of a silent system within their radial gaols was wildly out of tune with the post-Macmillan philosophy of rehabilitation. As liberal and laudatory an idea as this no doubt appeared, the 'dispersal' subsystem spawned by society's sudden concern for decent and humane containment, was, and still is, an expensive and ill-conceived disaster. There was without question a need for modern purpose built prisons. The abolition of the death penalty, coupled with an alarming predilection on the part of the judges to pass longer and longer sentences, led to a sharp increase in the number of long term prisoners in the already overstretched and overcrowded penal infrastructure. But the solution to 'disperse' the inmates from their local prisons to these new isolated institutions created a core of 'super criminals' out of an otherwise disorganised, disenfranchised rabble; for it allowed hardened criminals from, say, Manchester, Liverpool or Leeds, to associate quite freely with other hardened criminals from London, Bristol, Birmingham or wherever, for the very first time. In any profession, a gathering of the elite leads to an exchange of ideas. The criminal fraternity proved no less prone to talking shop, and very quickly, a whole new national network (now international with the influx of Irish, Palestinians and Libyans into the system) of underworld contact and co-operation came into being.

'Dispersal' prisons become then, the 'nuclear submarines' of our metaphorical fleet. In them, long underwater voyages of self-discovery are taken in the most closely confined quarters. Gone now are the spacious atria of Victoriana and the extravagant monumentality of their discredited dystopias. We were well into the New Elizabethan Age, where sixties modernism was seen as the natural way ahead. Perhaps the Department of the Environment's nightmare headquarters would be the most visible civilian equivalent of prisons within the 'dispersal' system. Or the Aylesbury Estate, south-east London. I suppose it depends in which circles you move. Either example provides a useful stylistic comparison.

Invariably sited on barren plains throughout the shires of England, they manifest the most 'functional' outward appearance of our three defined types. Their blandness lulls the mind into a gradual state of bored inertia; real wolves in sheep's clothing.

Wrapped in their concrete, perennially water-stained walls; crisscrossed with miles of razor-wired fencing; and sheltering smugly under the ultimate anti-escape devices – highly strung threads of orange, red and yellow balloons to stop invasion by helicopter; an archipelago of identical living blocks cluster around the prison's main office and communal facilities. Travel to the Isle of Wight to look at Albany, as far away from a set of rooms in

Piccadilly as the length of time it takes to make this journey across the Solent in heavy steel handcuffs. Or egress for the day to Long Lartin in the Vale of Evesham. Tarry at Gartree in Leicestershire if you will. At all these sites you will be rewarded by a glimpse of our 'nuclear submarines'.

Inside the stalagian time-capsules, an undercurrent of pervading violence seems all the more apparent because of closest confinement. The uniformly single cells, arranged in groups of eight or ten along spurs leading out of a central stairwell, are nothing more than tiny, almost square Inigo Jones cube-rooms. Square: $8 \times 8 \times 8$ feet; from end to end, a foot and a half longer than the screwed down turquoise beds. Outside your home terrain, there exists a forced intimacy and over exaggerated politeness with and towards other prisoners. You live and let live, or the heavily charged cannister explodes, and someone, occasionally, succumbs to murder in the air.

Surprisingly, I was always able to do my best academic work in this debilitating world. Graham Greene once noted that boredom bred creativity, and I think it is true that after the *Sturm und Drang* of everyday survival, the nightly lock-up in my cube-room was a welcome relief – an opportunity to escape into a world of my own where I could write far into the night, spewing out my thoughts onto the page, cleansing my system of the poison that particular day had emitted. Sometimes, If you lay awake very late, you might catch the faint sound of Beethoven's *Apassionata*, being played on a guitar on the other side of the cell wall. Or you might, on your evening rounds, stumble into another man's surreal oils seraglio, a cell crammed with strange organic shapes on canvasses created out of the nothingness of the night hours. Drug induced? Probably. Soft drugs were ubiquitous in this submerged world; and if you didn't create, you withered away.

About the same time as the 'dispersal' prisons appeared, our third category of type, the open and semi-open establishments, literally opened their gates to prisoners with low security ratings. Coracles, or rowing boats open to the sky, floating around the 'dispersals' with passenger sirens urging the 'submariner' to surface for a breath of fresh air, they are quintessentially nothing more than metamorphosed army and air force camps, playing the game of crime and punishment with other people's lives.

Architecturally, we're back in the 1940s, although at times one can even catch fleeting glimpses of the last days of the Indian Raj. Abandoned officers' rooms chopped into small dormitories live again behind their pseudo-Lutyens 'Queen Anne' facades. Deserted aircraft hangars have been converted into gloomy but capacious indoor sports centres. Peeling white flagpoles bend to the wind, and everywhere Nissen huts have been erected between trim lawns and fantastically coloured beds of summer bedding out plants.

Psychologically, the prisoner moves back to his childhood when faced with the pernickety regimes. He soon learns that within his apparent freedom, he must report here, there, everywhere, at impossibly difficult times, to a succession of different parades, roll calls, dining halls, workshops, welfare offices, wages huts, and even formally laid out kit inspections. I dare say all this is necessary (for the 'prison' must be seen to retain a modicum of discipline – these are after all places of punishment), but it does provoke in the prisoner a resentment of authority which led, in my own case, to an early morning of 'ghosting' from idyllic Highpoint in Suffolk, and my eventual return to the rigours and radiating spokes of Wandsworth.

Space will not allow me to draw any more than a brief vignette of an architecturally significant gaol of considerable historical importance. I mention it anyway, because being imprisoned there enabled me to partake in an unforgettable feast of visual splendour. High above the royal city of Lancaster, the eleventh-century castle forms part of a prison occupying the site of the old Roman Castrum. Built over Saxon foundations, financed by Roger de Poitou, damaged in the fourteenth century by Robert the Bruce, and restored and strengthened in the fifteenth century by John of Gaunt; the square stone keep now houses the association (leisure) rooms of prisoners serving their sentences in this extraordinary 700-year-old prison.

We lived in the shell of a round Norman tower, sleeping in trapezoidal cells arranged on four levels around its circumference. Access to this segmentalised accommodation was gained by climbing a central spiral staircase. From the cell windows, the view over the battlements was always grand and spectacular. For the superstitious, there were stories of Plantagenet ghosts and headless corpses buried in the castle walls. It was a forbidding and awesome place. I went back there not so long ago. It still is.

Throughout this essay, which barely breaks the surface of our secret existence, I have tried to give the reader an insight into a world of opposites – one that can inspire unique aesthetic highs, or destroy the soul completely. Nobody who has spent any serious length of time in prison would claim to have emerged without having gone through some degree of psychological pain along the line. Imprisonment *is* a traumatic experience, as the suicide statistics illustrate. Improvements in accommodation, sanitation and communication with the outside world are slowly (and belatedly; one thinks of the Strangeways riot) being made. Indeed, as I write this piece, I am 'fortunate' enough to be sitting in Bristol prison (a Victorian radial type with brutalist gatehouse), proper flush lavatory and sink *en suite*. It is still the same old railway carriage cell of course, and some would say that the installation of in-house plumbing is a double-edged sword giving screws the excuse they need to keep the prisoner in his cell for even longer periods at a time. But across the landing from my now locked door is another, up until recently, unheard of facility inside – a bank of public telephones. To be able to pick up one of those handsets and to hear the voices of loved ones at home . . .

Now there's the most humane prison innovation of the century.

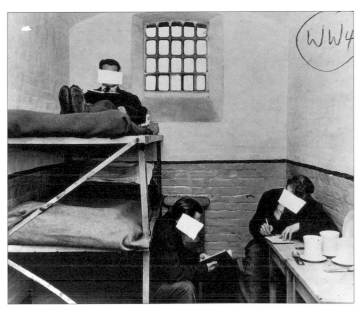

FROM ABOVE: Arrival of the Prisoners, Lancaster Castle, c1825 *(courtesy of Lancaster City Museums); cell interior with three prisoners,1961*

Prison Design in the Twentieth Century

Leslie Fairweather

The nineteenth-century inheritance

After centuries of squalor, brutality and corruption in prisons throughout the world, reforms during the eighteenth and nineteenth centuries led to gradual improvements in design and the treatment of offenders in many countries. By the mid-nineteenth century a more organised pattern of designs and regimes was evolving, especially in America and Europe, which was to dominate penal thinking for the next 100 years.

Generally, it was the radial type prison stemming from solitary confinement which dominated Europe – exemplified by the Eastern Penitentiary of Pennsylvania at Cherry Hill. More popular in America was the Auburn/'Silent System' layout, manifested clearly in Sing Sing prison. Under this regime long tiers of inside cells were arranged back-to-back, with open grilles facing on to the access galleries to allow light and ventilation, but little privacy. By the turn of the century there were thousands of both types of prison in use, which have shaped the structure of the penal system each country has inherited.

Pentonville Prison, opened in 1842, was the archetypal radial design in England. By 1848 there were 54 radial prisons based on this model either built or under construction throughout the country. In other European countries a similar type of radial architecture dominated to the same degree. The only breakaway design to emerge was a new prison layout known, for obvious reasons, as 'Telephone' pole: the plan shape resembled the central post (corridor) and crossbars (cell blocks) of a telephone pole. The first one was built at Fresnes in France in 1898. The use of one central control point – the hub of a radial prison – was thus rejected in favour of separate controls in each cell block.

This layout, in combination with varying designs of cell blocks, became popular in America and, to a lesser extent in Europe. It was to become more favoured again during this century when the radial principle became largely outmoded. By about 1920 there was still a preponderance of the two main forms of layout, plus a smattering of telephone-pole designs. But in addition, and in smaller numbers, were various other forms of architecture including: self-enclosed prisons, where the buildings themselves formed the perimeter walls; prisons arranged around one or more courtyards; open campus, or 'cottage' prisons; 'free' or open layouts, with buildings more casually sited in the landscape; panopticons, modern versions of the original Bentham idea, most of which were in America, though Europe had three and, strangely enough, they were all in The Netherlands (all three are still in use, as are many of the American examples); skyscraper prisons, again mostly built in America.

A later refinement in many American prisons was to build varying degrees of security within one institution. It also became increasingly common to design blocks with cells ranged along outside walls (as in radial prisons) rather than back-to-back in the middle of the blocks with open grilles and no direct air. Multiple variations on all these arrangements still abound: some successful, some of doubtful value. But all have influenced prison management and design during the past 50 years, playing an important role in the development of correctional institutions. Finally, rising dissatisfaction with its obsolescent prison stock led to a fundamental rethink in America, which once again provided a lead to the rest of the world.

America seizes the initiative

Increasing frustration at the barrenness and futility of much of their prison heritage led American administrators and architects to take stock. In 1930, the Federal Bureau of Prisons was established and set new standards for prison design and construction. In 1949, the Bureau issued a *Handbook of Correctional Design and Construction* with later supplements, which was influential throughout the world in improving quality. More recently, the National Clearing House for Criminal Justice Planning and Architecture was established in the Department of Architecture, University of Illinois. Its massive publication *Guidelines for the Planning and Design of Regional and Community Correctional Centres for Adults* attempted a fresh look at the functions and purposes of every aspect of prison life and design. The chief lessons learnt by the Americans were that:

– there had been an almost complete failure of any form of rehabilitation because of excessive prison size, overbearing security and supervision, and gross overcrowding

– more sophisticated methods of assessment and evaluation of a prisoner's needs had to be devised; possibly resulting in alternative means of remedial treatment such as community service

– research must discover how to spend money more wisely on criminal justice. Americans were spending more on household pets than on the police; more on tobacco than on the whole criminal justice system

– easy supervision of inmates was not the only goal

– prisons should be smaller; existing prisons were holding from 1,000 to 5,000 inmates

– prisons should be within centres of population

- prisons must be flexible; environment and scale should be as 'normal' as possible
- better security systems and zoning should allow for more individual freedom within the institution
- proper workshops, recreation, visiting and educational facilities must be provided
- internal layouts should afford maximum contact between staff and inmates to allow as much individual contact and treatment as possible.

Other influences were at work, including the first ever International Study Group on Prison Architecture, held in London during July 1961, attended by administrators and architects from 13 countries worldwide. It was the first occasion when participating professionals could exchange experiences and learn from each other. Another input was the research carried out by the United Nations Social Defence Research Institute in Rome (UNSDRI, since renamed the United Nations Interregional Crime and Justice Research Institute UNICRI). This resulted, in 1975, in a massive tome *Prison Architecture,* which contained analytical articles, plus scale plans and details of 27 prisons from 14 countries. These and other influences had a considerable impact on attitudes to penal reform, nowhere more so than in America.

The breakthrough came in the 1970s when a concept known as 'New Generation' was born in America. The term did not refer to design as such, but to new ways of managing prisons, to which design must respond. In essence, the prisons were subdivided into small groups of inmates each in the care of multi-disciplinary teams of staff, with responsibility to run their units in their own way. The earlier aims of therapy and rehabilitation were transmuted into ways of helping inmates to change and improve as a result of their own efforts. This was an old nineteenth-century idea, but instead of a loom, a treadmill and a bible, prisoners were given a range of work and other incentives, with a system of privileges or punishments depending on how they behaved or responded. The idea was to divide prisoners into three main types, each accommodated in separate housing units.

The first group consisted of the hostile, aggressive, psychopathic agitators: the 'victimisers'. The second group contained the so-called 'normals': the prisoners who would do their time and cause no trouble. In the third group were the 'victims': the inadequates, the dependants, the neurotics and the anxious.

Any of these prisoners could be transferred up or down a series of security grades between or within prisons, from the very secure to the very open depending on their behaviour. The architecture which resulted avoided long grey cell corridors and tall galleries, and replaced them with small groups of cells arranged in only two levels around multi-use communal areas. Staff could control inmates less conspicuously and foster better personal relationships; and prisoners could be allowed considerable freedom of movement. Each cell had its own sanitation and a window to the outside air. Decorations and furnishings in these

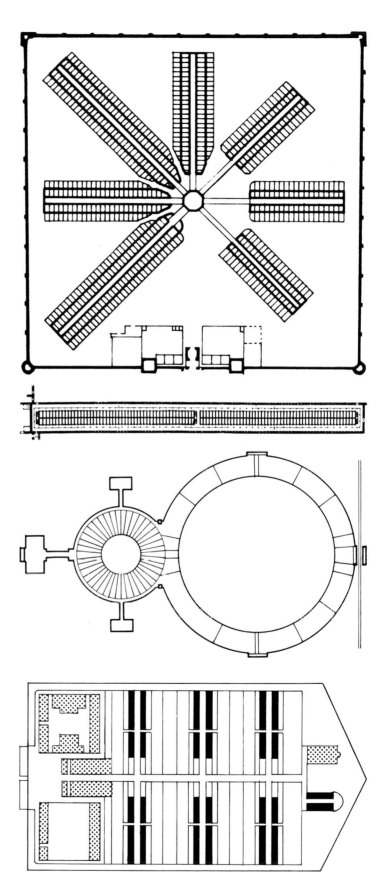

FROM ABOVE: *Eastern Penitentiary of Pennsylvania: the basic plan and section shape for all other 'Pennsylvania' prisons; Sing Sing Prison plan which established the design for other Auburn/Sing Sing types; New Ohio State Penitentiary plan: the project was never realised; first telephone-pole prison at Fresnes, France*

new prisons were cheerful and attractive, interiors light and airy, and noise levels kept low. The aim was to give each prisoner a sense of place within a large institution, accommodated in separate and identifiable housing units, each with its own style of management. A more relaxed atmosphere with a clear sense of commitment and purpose were among the benefits claimed.

A more complete contrast to everything that had gone before would be hard to imagine. The lessons of the past had been well and truly learned, but the question has to be asked whether they provide any better results, and whether they are actually being used in the ways intended?

New Generation takes hold

The basic design which emerged from this 'Small is Beautiful' transformation was a series of triangular units, containing small groups of cells on two levels around a central multi-use association space. Because each cell opens directly on to the central association area, staff can observe all the cells and the inmates without making it too obvious they are doing so. The idea of smaller groups was adopted with enthusiasm. What took longer to accept was the whole raison d'être of New Generation prisons: a more relaxed relationship and more direct communication between staff and inmates. Removing the paraphernalia of security grilles and remote control locking systems was psychologically demanding on both staff and inmates. Professionals involved in the operation of prisons are by no means unanimous in their acceptance of these new principles which some find threatening, as do some prisoners.

Although the triangular form of cell block (either singly or coupled in pairs) has dominated most of the American New Generation prison layouts, it is by no means universal. A whole variety of shapes has been developed: cruciforms, stars, clusters, courtyards, rectangles, slabs, semi-circles, even trouser-shaped. But they all share the common property of smaller groups of inmates accommodated in more intimate housing units, within an overall institution size of 400 to 500. House units can vary in size from six to 70 occupants, with an average of between 24 and 36. This is in stark contrast to the many hundreds herded together in the older galleried prisons. The houses (or cell blocks) are usually not physically linked by corridor to the other facilities or to each other; each house group being reached off a 'business street' by open paths across a landscaped community green.

If larger prisons are needed, they tend to be subdivided into separate units within the campus, possibly with varying degrees of security, each surrounded by double wire fences. The Federal Correctional Complex at Allenwood, Pennsylvania is a good example of this type. It consists of three main institutions with differing degrees of security, housing a total of 2,300 inmates. Each of the institutions is quite different in design, but all are based on small group principles. However, one of the institutions is more tightly designed with corridor access (not open paths)

surrounding the cell blocks; the corridor forming the outer perimeter wall. This latter type of design can be found in some other new American prisons, which are joined horizontally by (sometimes very long) corridors; eg, at Florence; Pittsburgh; Erie County; Maury, North Carolina; Hillsborough; and Minnesota.

Urban prisons tend to consist of clusters of cells connected vertically by stairs and lifts, eg Foley Square, New York; Kenosha, Wisconsin; and Miami. All prisons now include generous central facilities – the business and community focus of the institution – containing administration and visiting rooms, vocational training and industry workshops, central dining rooms and prisoners' shop, recreation areas and a gymnasium and sports field. Dining may be in a common dining hall for the whole institution, or served in the house units by trolley from a central kitchen.

Construction tries to mirror, as far as possible, the vernacular buildings of the locality in terms of massing, scale and detailing. Materials tend to be brick, stucco and glass with sloping metal roofs. Reinforced concrete and cladding is often used for tall buildings. Extensive use of prefabrication, in terms of large elements made in a factory and assembled on site, is more rare.

These types of New Generation prison still represent 'state of the art' design and are by no means representative of the many thousands of institutions throughout the range of existing provision in the United States. The majority of Federal, State and County facilities are in older buildings with large, long cell blocks containing hundreds of back-to-back internal cells in three or four layers.

The Federal system is now wedded to this new idea of unit management. But elsewhere State and County prisons and gaols are commonly run on more traditional lines. Opinion is divided in America about how successful the New Generation principles are proving to be. Practice has not always reflected theory, especially in the intended degree of close inmate/staff contact. Prisons are labour intensive and labour is expensive. At a time of huge capital investment, the high staffing ratio demanded by New Generation prisons may be unrealistic, adding considerably to the operational costs. One way of reducing staffing levels is to operate a less 'hands on' policy by more remote supervision and more use of electronic locking and control systems, especially in the super-maximum security institutions. The perceived degree of control is crucial to the safety and reassurance of staff and inmates. Some inmates and staff feel physically threatened by the potential for violence in the large open communal spaces; prison officers may retreat into the more protective and comforting environment of remote control that they know and are more at ease with. Violent prisoners could actually be worse off in such an open environment, and have less freedom of movement with more physical restraints imposed when taken out of their cells.

There seems no doubt, however, about the wisdom of segregating inmates into different categories in smaller units, not only for convenience but for the safety of certain groups of prisoners such as sex offenders and informers who frequently suffer violence at the hands of other prisoners. Classifying prisoners into groups implies an over-supply of cells so that there will always be space within any one group for new inmates. Prison sizes and sentencing policies have to be balanced to take account of this. The New Generation institutions will need very careful monitoring over the years to discover whether their high hopes and ideals are being realised or whether they are, realistically, actually realisable. While the American experience is extremely valuable, other countries should be wary about copying their methods and designs too closely.

There are two additional features of American policy worth noting. The first is that it has a large enough prison building programme to allow for experimentation. This is also of value to smaller countries which can benefit from the results of such experiments. The second is that the architects have greater freedom and encouragement to produce innovative designs and speedier and cheaper building methods. The sheer scale of America's problems is daunting. In one year, its increase in prison population equalled the total prison population of the United Kingdom at that time. It has a crisis over increasingly violent and drugs-related crimes, such that there will never be enough prisons to accommodate those sentenced by the courts under current legislation. Parole is being eliminated from the US Federal justice system, thus exacerbating an already serious overcrowding problem, and partly negating the use of 'cascading' whereby a prisoner can, by good behaviour, improve his lot by transferring to more salubrious accommodation. There will come a time when he has gone as far as he can go and will be unable to see any further advantage in being good. Not only will prison populations grow larger, they will grow older and stay longer.

State expenditure on correctional institutions causes some to believe that if they build the prisons needed they could not also afford schools, welfare and medical aid. Cost throws up a difficult equation. The National Institute of Justice reckoned that a typical prison inmate (in 1988), if not locked up, would commit 187 crimes a year at a total cost of $430,000 a year. Yet, claims the Institute, it costs only $25,000 a year to keep him in prison. The problem with this line of reasoning is that it depends on the detection and conviction rate, the rising capital costs of building prisons, and the operating costs which are largely dependent on numbers of prison staff. Even so, incarceration is not the answer for many thousands of offenders, and the deterrence factor of prison has been found to be extremely low. Other methods are being constantly explored and of the roughly three million people under some kind of correctional supervision in America, less than 20 per cent are in prisons.

The United Kingdom catches up

Like many other countries, there has been confusion in the UK about what prisons are actually for: what they are intended to achieve. Under Gladstone, their purpose was deterrence and

FROM ABOVE: *Clusters of cell blocks at West County Justice Center, Contra Costa County, California; linked series of triangular cell blocks with corridor access at Erie County Jail, Pennsylvania; urban prison at Kenosha, Wisconsin, with cell blocks arranged vertically in groups*

reformation. The only trouble was that they neither deterred nor reformed. Rehabilitation was tried in the 1960s, but was shown to have no effect at all on recidivism (the number of times a prisoner is reconvicted). 'Humane containment' was all the rage in the early 1970s. This did at least shift the emphasis from what happened after a prisoner left, to what he or she did while actually serving the sentence. However, all these aims led to disillusionment and cynicism and to pejorative phrases like 'human warehouses' and 'penal dustbins'. Clearly, a new realism was called for in the 1990s, with a more encouraging attitude to the treatment of offenders, and a more innovative approach to the design of institutions.

Judge Tumim has more recently restated the purpose of the prison service as the need: first, to keep prisoners securely; second, to look after them with humanity; third, to help them lead law-abiding and useful lives in custody and after release.

The UK prison inheritance, in terms of buildings and regimes, has not always encouraged such aims. A large proportion of the prisons stem from the model radial prison at Pentonville built in 1842. Here, the architecture precisely matched the purposes of strict isolation, hard labour and moral introspection as a means of reform and salvation, combined with total ease of supervision by a minimum of staff.

After a spate of radial prison building during the middle to end of the nineteenth-century nothing much happened until the opening of a security training prison, Everthorpe Hall, in Yorkshire in 1958. But the design was a close imitation of the nineteenth century prisons and was out of date before it even left the drawing board. This forced the Home Office to take design more seriously to cater for the new prison building programme announced in the 1959 government White Paper *Changing Practice in a Changing Society*. As a result, a 'new wave' of 22 prisons appeared around the country over the next few years, the first being at Blundeston in Suffolk. Gone were the long open-tiered cell blocks on the radial pattern; instead, the new housing units had separate, solid floors and were designed to contain smaller groups of prisoners. The units were attached to a central nucleus of communal facilities. In other prisons cell blocks, either singly or in pairs, were linked by corridors to the rest of the prison, often imitating telephone-pole layouts. A training workshop and sports ground were contained within the perimeter fence. Other designs developed, such as cells ranged around open courtyards, often for no discernible architectural reason or sound penal principle.

In the early 1970s, there was a total halt on prison expenditure in the UK – designs were ready but there was no cash. By the time the programme got under way again in 1979, the designs taken off the shelf were six years old. Thus, all the 1980s prisons were already out of date. In 1984 the government published a report *Managing the Long Term Prison System*. This shifted the emphasis from control of the prison to the needs of the prisoner.

It implied a greater flexibility of programmes and designs to suit different individuals, while questioning the basic assumptions about what should be happening in penal establishments. This was followed, at the end of 1985, by a further Home Office report *A Sense of Direction* which announced, quite firmly, that 'activity is the key to a good prison: an idle prisoner is a dangerous prisoner'. Activity was seen as one part of a trinity of principles; the other two being 'individualism' and 'relationships'.

Starting with the precept that imprisonment itself is the punishment, the key issue was seen as the relationship between the individual prisoner and the individual member of staff. These conceptual shifts in direction influenced and coincided with similar changes in design approach. The report drew attention to the recent developments in the United States: the New Generation. Later that year a Home Office working party went over to see what lessons could be learned for the UK. On its return the working party wrote a report *New Directions in Prison Design* which analysed the eight prisons visited and drew conclusions for the UK, in matching together management aims and design.

The publication did not come a moment too soon, for the 25th report of the House of Commons Committee of Public Accounts had just been severely critical of many aspects of the prison system and its buildings, urging that the costly mistakes of the 1960s and 1970s be avoided. Those mistakes were only too self-evident: long corridors with no natural light gave an institutionalised atmosphere which inhibited staff/inmate contact. Too many corners made supervision difficult and staff did not feel secure. Manning levels were high, and therefore costly. There were too many expensive design and construction faults. The Home Office realised that a totally new commitment had to be made if the building programme was to have any chance of success, allowing more appropriate designs to emerge.

All this led, in 1987, to a dedicated design team being set up in the Prison Department with a requirement to produce within one year design briefs which would more precisely establish Home Office requirements, design principles, standards of provision and cost limits based on current policy requirements. They were to update earlier briefing guides (first produced in 1976 and by then obsolete), and incorporate the lessons learned from the British and American experiences.

To make such a study possible in the time, it was restricted to the requirements of a medium-security (category B) training prison for 600 adult males. But it was also applicable to other types of establishment and provided a comprehensive and rationalised database for the design of all types of institution.

The resultant design briefs were a splendid multi-disciplinary achievement in such a short space of time. The Prison Design Briefing System (PDBS) was published in the form of a series of booklets (at first 27, since increased to over 40) analysing every prison function. Each booklet contained a statement of Prison Department requirements, a description of the design and planning implications, and analytical illustrations showing how the requirements might be met. The design sketches were not meant to be standard building solutions: the guidance was intended to be flexible and not prescriptive. PDBS did not offer firm design solutions but created a benchmark against which other designs could be measured. Emphasis was on achieving as 'normal' an environment as possible, consistent with security; on encouraging more fruitful interrelationships between prisoners and staff; and on understanding the activities which go on in prisons.

The PDBS design suggestions showed a grouping of residential accommodation around a green recreational area, linked by a prison street containing shops, visiting facilities, chapel and education centre. A short walk away were the workshops and sports fields. Of key importance to the design of the prison were the inmate housing units (or cell blocks) where the idea of the American New Generation design was adopted but not the triangular shapes. Every housing unit consisted of two levels of 24 to 30 cells grouped in a rectangle around a day association space, with a central glazed observation room shared with a similar, but separate, adjoining unit. A possible criticism of this design, as with nearly all the American triangular examples, is that the central association space is too enclosed and claustrophobic with no view to the outside.

There was no resemblance between these new PDBS ideas and the old Victorian galleried prisons, or even the more recent Blundeston-type corridor designs. Although the PDBS recommended rectangular cell blocks, in fact three prisons were built with triangular shaped housing units as in the American examples: at Milton Keynes, Doncaster and Lancaster Farms.

Milton Keynes afforded outward views from the association area: with one complete side glazed and not enclosed. The other two prisons only allow slits of light. These three designs are unlikely to be repeated in the UK as triangular shapes are more costly to build and their very mannered geometry produces complex building junctions. But whatever shape the cell blocks may be, smaller groups of inmates held in smaller scale units, will be the guiding principles for all future new and refurbished prisons in the UK. The American New Generation prisons and the equivalent UK institutions designed to PDBS standards both present the staff with more responsibility, particularly the prison officers. Much depends on the degree of independent control each unit is allowed, on how carefully the prison officers are trained and how creatively they react. It will be instructive to compare the American and British experiences.

The new ideas had to be introduced into an existing UK building programme and it was decided to continue with the building of five new galleried prisons, already designed. Two of the early ones were built at Woolwich and Bullingdon in Oxfordshire. They were cruciform in shape and much smaller in scale than the old Victorian radial prisons but, in essence, were very similar. The layout was still over-directional and the

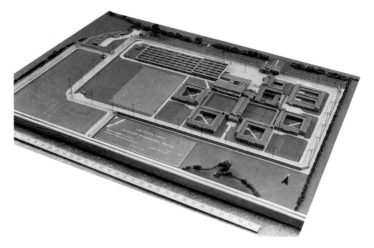

FROM ABOVE: *Association space in one of the triangular cell blocks at Woodhill Prison, Milton Keynes; Blundeston Prison, Suffolk, the first of the new wave of prisons with separate cell blocks; Low Newton, Durham, a typical courtyard prison*

custodial atmosphere inhibited easy interaction but, it must be said, they seem popular with prison staff who are more accustomed to that type of layout. A further disadvantage of cruciform, triangular or radial shapes is that they are more difficult to fit into tight sites than rectangles.

While preparations continued for an enlarged programme of new PDBS prisons, and drastic refurbishment of the older stock, a calamity occurred. The worst riots in the history of the UK prison service tore apart the fragile truce which exists between those who suffer incarceration and those whose duty it is to enforce it.

Prison riots accelerate change

For 25 days in April 1990, riots broke out in six prisons of which the most notorious casualty was Strangeways prison in Manchester. So serious were the outbreaks that the Home Secretary ordered an enquiry into the disturbances, headed by Lord Justice Woolf and Judge Stephen Tumim. Their 600 page report was presented to Parliament in February 1991 and sparked off a flurry of activity. It made a number of recommendations:
- the largest prisons should hold only 400 inmates accommodated in smaller and more manageable units of between 50 and 70 inmates. Designs for both new and refurbished prisons should follow the guidelines set out in the PDBS
- there should be a careful balance between security and oppression
- prisons should be community-based to maintain close links with the prisoners' families and with the local population
- remand prisoners should be accommodated in separate units or separate prisons
- each prisoner should be entitled to a separate cell
- prisoners should at all times have access to sanitation. 'Slopping out' should end by February 1996.

The ensuing White Paper *Custody Care and Justice* claimed 'to chart a course for the Prison Service for the rest of this century and beyond'. It embodied most of the recommendations in the Woolf Report, but did not meet with universal approbation. The Prison Reform Trust, for example, referred to its 'half-hearted language' and its 'failure to tackle the problem of prison overcrowding' which the Trust claimed 'put the future success of the reforms in doubt'. But it did admit that, 'beneath the slick surface, the White Paper represents a considerable advance for prison reform'. An immediate start was made on refurbishing and extending Strangeways Prison and repairing the damage to the other riot prisons. Fitting cells with integral sanitation was speeded up, plus considerable improvements, extensions and plans to combat severe overcrowding throughout the prison estate. But very few new prisons will be constructed for the foreseeable future (except by private enterprise).

The Prison Department is now concentrating most of its £200 million annual budget on bringing the old prisons up to scratch. Apart from the prisons at Milton Keynes, Doncaster and Lancaster

Farms, only one new prison has recently been completed: at Buckley Hall in Rochdale. This institution is a medium security (Category C) prison holding 300 inmates designed to PDBS standards. The cell blocks are rather narrower than suggested in the PDBS model designs, for the site is very sloping and the slimmer blocks slot more comfortably into the steep contours. The whole complex was built in 15 months, from inception to completion: an incredibly short time for a prison, made possible by a prefabricated system of construction. Groups of four cells at a time, complete with plumbing, windows and doors, were manufactured in workshops and brought by lorries for assembly on site. Design and construction was carried out by the Home Office Prison Department. This is likely to be the last new prison to be directly under the control of the Prison Department, which will now concentrate chiefly on refurbishment and additions to existing prisons.

New prisons, in the future, will be let to private contract under an arrangement known as DCMF (Design, Construction, Management, Financing). Thus total responsibility for the building and running of the institution will be taken over by private contractors. However, all the preliminary feasibility work and assessment will be carried out by the Prison Department, which will also retain overall charge of letting the contracts and monitoring the results at all stages. Administration of the completed prison will also be subject to strict regulation and inspection, like any other prison in the system. The designs will need to be based on the principles laid down in the PDBS, but there will be scope for innovation and amendment.

Two designs were originally prepared (for buildings at Ashford, Middlesex, and Kirkham) which matched exactly the model designs drawn in the PDBS handbooks. But neither yet has full planning consent or site clearance. Sites, at Fazakerley, Liverpool and Bridge End in South Wales, have been acquired, and other sites are being investigated. But, although the Home Secretary announced a programme of six new prisons, at an estimated cost of £500 million, none can be built until private money is available under the DCMF scheme. If private investors cannot be found, none will be built.

Every country is concerned at the rising costs of building and managing prisons; the UK is no exception. While the PDBS remains the benchmark, its recommendations will have to be weighed against the need to cut both capital and operating costs. This may take the form of reduced staffing levels or changes in design to make management easier, but without compromising the needs and rights of inmates and staff. Economic operating costs are crucial and will increasingly affect design and construction. Decisions taken in the early stages of design can have a major impact on efficiency and (with privatisation) on profitability.

The UK prison building programme, apart from huge improvements to existing establishments, is thus now waiting for private investors to pick up the tab. Until they do, there will be no new prisons built. Such an *ad hoc* policy cannot respond to demand, nor encourage an integrated rolling investment programme of refurbished and new build prisons.

The idea of privatisation, and encouraging a competitive element into the running of UK prisons, has gained strength over a very short time span. When first mooted, the Home Secretary of the day expressed little confidence in the idea. But within five years any qualms have been overcome and now privatisation is seen as the most appropriate way forward; as part and parcel of the government's general approach to public sector management. The first of the new privatised prisons was opened at the Wolds, Humberside, in 1992. Others have followed.

Some reform groups remain uneasy and insist that there must be less secrecy and greater accountability with, in particular, protection of prisoners' rights. American experience is yet too small and novel to offer much guidance. Only about 1 per cent of US prisons are privatised but one of the market leaders, the Corrections Corporation of America, is a partner in the UK consortium which runs the second privatised prison, at Blakenhurst, near Birmingham. Interestingly, the bid for managing and operating the refurbished and extended Strangeways prison was won by the Prison Service itself.

Problems worldwide

Rising crime rates have led to an almost insatiable demand for more prison places. Each country tackles its problems in its own way, drawing on the experience of others. It is not possible in the space available to cover developments in every other country in the world. What follows, therefore, is a flavour of prison design.

CANADA

Like many other countries, Canada has moved from an environment of communal penitence before the 1940s, to attempts at simulating community living in the 1990s. Early prisons, not surprisingly, were very similar to those of its close neighbour, the United States. Then, during the 1950s, institutions were split into smaller groups, with larger cells affording a view to the world outside. However, the 1960s saw a major programme of prison building and improvement, adding about 4,000 new beds. Many new Federal prisons each accommodating an average of 450 inmates, were built to higher security levels and designed to limit not encourage staff/inmate contact. Separate staff corridors and remote control in 'bubbles' were standard features. The prisons stressed efficiency and, it has been claimed, 'were, to a large extent, driven by the detention equipment industry'.

A typical example is the maximum security prison at Millhaven, completed in 1967 with 447 inmates. The institution is totally enclosed by its own buildings, plus a double security fence. The cell blocks take the shape of interlinked radials, with cells on the upper floor (in groups of 29) and exercise areas on the floor

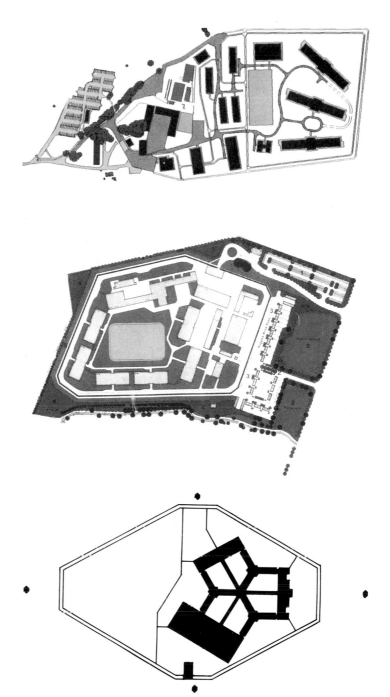

FROM ABOVE: *Buckley Hall Prison, Rochdale; design for a PDBS prison at Ashford; Millhaven maximum security prison, Canada: a mixture of three radials and six courtyards*

below. The lower security prisons were more open in character, with 'X'-shaped cell blocks grouped around a garden. The institution at Cowansville, with 432 inmates, has a more relaxed layout, with a spread out campus of separate buildings connected by long corridors.

The smaller cell blocks house only 17 inmates per floor. These earlier designs resulted in considerable alienation, and new approaches to lessen confrontation were attempted in the 1970s. This new direction initiated smaller, less austere institutions, incorporating more humane environments and encouraging more interaction between staff and inmates. The institution which best epitomises this change of heart is at Mission in British Columbia. The 180 inmates are grouped in 36 room units, split into two sections of 18, joined by a central activity space. The living rooms are arranged on two floors with nine rooms per floor, and with the activity space at mezzanine level opposite. Specially designed furniture was made by the inmates. A full range of other facilities in separate blocks, and a large sports field complete the site, which is surrounded by a double 4.3 metre fence. An unfortunate by-product of increased interaction between staff and inmates was found to be the opportunity it afforded inmates to pit staff one against the other.

Another prison of the time is the detention centre at Etobicoke, Ontario. Again small-scale, it holds 216 inmates in three security groups: maximum, minimum and temporary absence. Two 'L' shaped units of only ten cells each are clustered around day rooms to hold 20. It is a low profile, articulated brick structure on a sloping site and is certainly much less aggressive than many previous prison designs.

The mixed experience of the 1970s resulted in opposing views. Some held that the pendulum had swung too far and the staff needed greater protection; others that the more liberal view of prison as a community should be persevered with. Security in many prisons was upgraded with additional controls, and new institutions designed to minimise the risk of violence. But the Correctional Service of Canada achieved a few notable examples of gentler architecture, such as the Bowden Institution. Here, two-storey house units were 'H'-shaped, with five or ten beds per wing and general activity spaces in the middle, but variations were possible. A 'neighbourhood' might consist, for example, of 40 beds accommodated in four, six or eight houses within the total 'community' of 160. Square housing units were also developed with a double-height living area in the middle. More responsibility for their actions was given to the inmates.

The future will focus more on lower-security facilities and on using other methods than incarceration for offenders. Where institutions are built, housing will take the form of apartments or houses, each shared by five or six offenders. 'New Generation' principles are infiltrating the Canadian prison system but much will depend on whether the regime is found too threatening for staff and not effective enough for inmates.

SWEDEN

Traditional open-tiered cell blocks, either radial or 'T' shaped, dominated Swedish prisons during the nineteenth century. About 50 were built, of which 15 are still in use, mostly upgraded and converted. The Prisons Act of 1945 required individual treatment of offenders, after which Swedish institutions became smaller and more specialised. Some of the best were for youthful offenders, such as those at Skenäs, Roxtuna and Hällby. All were designed with small housing units containing only about ten boys. Layouts were informal and the grounds well landscaped. The buildings were moderate in scale and domestic in appearance. The prison hospital at Haga and prison at Hall were places of pilgrimage for many European prison administrators and architects after the Second World War when prison building programmes began to get under way again. Sweden then produced a few more new prisons, notably at Kumla and Tidaholm where a prison was sited around a factory. Kumla, with its long lines of cells, harsh finishes, and an underground tunnel linking the cell blocks, was a contrast to the earlier prisons, causing something of a furore. Such a preoccupation with prisoner control had not been the Swedish way of doing things.

In 1973, the prison system was more closely linked to the probation and parole service, and to agencies which would assist prisoners on release. One consequence of this was that prisoners would be moved, before their release, from the larger national institutions to more local ones. Those serving sentences of a year or less would go direct to a local institution, each of which accommodates about 40 inmates, both men and women. Separate accommodation is provided for women, but otherwise they share the same association and work areas with the men.

Some 25 institutions, which would otherwise have been suitable except for their age and condition, were replaced by new facilities over a period of 15 years. In 1980, a further 30 new local institutions were authorised. The regime is fairly relaxed with inmates often allowed out to use local recreational facilities. Living quarters are arranged in eight groups of five rooms each, allowing some degree of classification and segregation. Some prisons are open, others closed. The latter are obviously more carefully controlled to prevent escape and the smuggling in of narcotics and alcohol. Double wire netting fences, 3 metres high, surround the compounds. The emphasis at these local institutions is on readjustment not punishment. A typical example is at Taby, not far from Stockholm. Sweden's smaller population makes this size of institution possible; larger countries might not be able to afford such high staffing costs.

THE NETHERLANDS

One of the most enterprising building programmes in Europe has been under way in The Netherlands for the past decade, and is still continuing. The Dutch had to cope, like most countries, with an increasing number of offenders (many for drug-related crimes) coupled with an antiquated prison estate. The Dutch government, worried at the severe overcrowding, rejected any suggestion that prisoners should share cells. It embarked on a five-point plan by: reopening some of the older institutions; reclaiming administrative offices and converting them into cells; creating emergency places; modifying and enlarging existing prisons; building new correctional institutions.

The new prisons do not appear to have been influenced so far by American New Generation management principles, or by PDBS layouts. But future institutions may well adopt the idea of smaller groups in less formal surroundings. At least another 1,000 cells will be needed over the next few years, and it is admitted that new institutions 'will have to be constructed along more recent design specifications', with a capacity of 204 inmates each, and a limit to the number of static control points. One New Generation-style triangular prison is already on the drawing board, as an idea at least.

One of the first of the new wave of Dutch prisons was completed in Maastricht in 1975. It consists of eight floors of cells rising above a mainly two-storey podium, and with single and double-storey surrounding buildings containing administration, association rooms, workshops and kitchens. The cell block contains 24 cells per floor in two groups of 12, separated by a control point and lobby. Total accommodation is for 231 inmates, both men and women. Cells face outwards, with a saw-tooth window profile to prevent overlooking. This device was used in Stuttgart-Stammheim prison and in Woodhill prison, Milton Keynes (and also in Coventry Cathedral, but for a very different purpose!). However, the extra costs and complications involved would seem to outweigh the rather doubtful benefits.

The more recent Dutch prisons are very similar to each other in concept and vary only in detail. They mostly retain traditional tiers of cells in open halls, but are smaller in overall capacity and in the sizes of cell groups, than has been usual in the past. Experiments have been made in the sectional shape of some cell blocks, which tend to be more adventurous than the plans. While a form of open gallery access is normal, the facing walls are sometimes glazed with sloping glass (as in Rotterdam) or have curved window walls (as at Hoorn). The prison at Rotterdam has been nicknamed 'The Golden Sphinx' for its impressive gold-tinted sloping walls.

Most other new Dutch prisons are flat roofed, with or without some form of roof lights. The prison at Lelystad has a huge central glazed dome. The plans are inward looking with cells facing inner courtyards used for sports and recreation. This type of plan also provides good perimeter security, but it can lead to excessively long corridors and circulation routes, and inflexibility. Maximum capacity is around 252 cells, but sometimes as low as 144. In general, cells are subdivided into units of about 24 each. They are usually arranged fairly traditionally along two or three tiers of open galleries, with 24 cells in each tier.

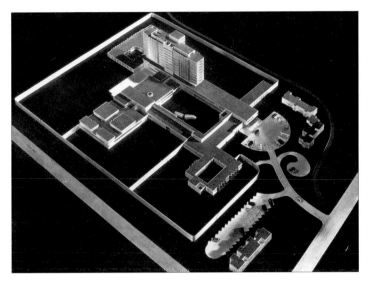

FROM ABOVE: *The security wall of Kumla Prison, Sweden; Maastricht Prison, The Netherlands: cells are mainly in the tall block (photograph: Jacques Huinck); Woodhill Prison, Milton Keynes with 'saw-tooth' wall of cells*

While most of the new Dutch prisons are designed around open courtyards, the actual layouts differ significantly, especially in the relationship of the cell blocks to the rest of the prison buildings. It goes without saying that all the new prisons have sanitation in each cell, and that association rooms, workshops and administration areas are provided on the site as a matter of course. The courtyard institutions can be roughly grouped into four types, ranging from one courtyard to four, as follows:

- 'U'-shaped plans with a single central courtyard and long banks of cells in three levels facing inwards, on both sides. The long arms of the court are connected mid-span by an overpass.

  A good example of this type is at Hoorn which can accommodate 192 prisoners, in 12 groups of 16 cells, with gallery access. Running parallel to the cells, and opposite to them at mezzanine level, are association rooms.

  There are variations on the single court theme. At Hoogeveen 252 cells line two sides of a 'U'-shaped block connected at the end by association rooms, with a sports field in the middle. Further along, workshops line two further courts, with administration buildings at the far end. The whole is surrounded by a perimeter wall. The prison also bears some resemblance to the institutions at Leeuwarden and Rotterdam.

  The 144 capacity cell block at Vught is within a totally enclosed single square courtyard. And a schematic design (not built) shows a circular cell block enclosing a central court, set within a square of associated prison buildings, thereby creating further courts at the corners.

- Rotterdam Remand Centre is another example of long banks of cells facing each other, but subdivided into two separate courts linked by association rooms, and sealed off at each end by workshops and administration. The inner courts are used for recreation and sport. This prison is larger: 252 cells arranged in long lines of 24 cells reached by open galleries.

- Three courtyards feature in the prison at Leeuwarden. The outer two are contained by 'L'-shaped cell blocks with the remaining two sides filled in by other prison buildings. Within the outer courts are general outdoor activity areas. The smaller central court is for sports. The 252 cells are in groups of 24 spread over three storeys. Another three courtyard plan is at Nijmegen, where cells are arranged facing only one side of each court, with maximum security accommodation and a long access corridor completing the other sides.

- The final courtyard layout is a simple cruciform cell block, with central access and outside cells, set within a square of other buildings and thus creating four separate courtyards at each corner. Sittard prison is an example of this type, with 252 cells arranged in groups of 24 over three floors. The four courts are used for sports and leisure. Another example is at Almelo with 144 cells. An intriguing mixture of cruciform and court can be found at Dordrecht, where the ground floor is part cruciform but with enclosed courtyards on two of the diagonals. The floor above loses the courts and is cruciform in shape. However, the cruciform design does not permit observation from a central hub, for the cells are in separate 'L'-shaped wings on the outer edges of the cross with no common axis. The basic plan is actually a series of 'L'-shaped cell modules which can be configured in a variety of ways.

There are more traditional plan layouts, as at Grave and Arnhem, with long lines of cells and open gallery access. A published scheme with triangular plan looks a possible precursor of a more fully-fledged PDBS or New Generation layout, although the whole prison is triangular with only one tip devoted to cells. At Lelystad, huge square cell blocks are surmounted by soaring glass domes over the central spaces.

The most imaginative idea is a study for a 144-cell penitentiary with an outer circular ring of cells, almost panopticon style but subdivided into three separate courts. Over that is a triangle, with inward sloping sides, containing another layer of cells in three rows of 24 cells, each around a central observation post. Crowning the top is another small ring of observation cells. It is structurally and spatially exciting – almost like a flying saucer – but difficult to predict how easy it would be to administer.

FRANCE

While the Dutch prisons maintain a general consistency of approach, French institutions are more varied in their architecture. One of the earliest of the new prisons is at Fleury Mérogis south of Paris. Built in 1968 and housing 2,886 inmates, it is possibly the largest in Europe. It contains, within the multifaceted workshop blocks and plant rooms which form its perimeter, five separate radial cell blocks.

Each five-storey block has three radiating wings of cells, with an average of 50 cells per level. Floors are solid and access to cells is from a corridor, which doubles up as communal recreation space. All available exterior spaces within the perimeter are used for exercise and sport. Two much smaller satellite compounds, containing one radial block each, are for detention of young adults and for women. Emphasis is entirely on control, security, economy and the processing of prisoners in the most convenient way. It is unlikely that such a huge prison will again be built in France: it runs totally counter to the current trend of small scale, flexible design and more personalised management.

It is appropriate that having introduced the telephone-pole plan layout to France (at Fresnes in 1898) another should have been built recently, at Chateauroux in 1972. It is a classic telephone-pole design, with cell blocks serviced by a connecting corridor and 384 cells arranged along three floors, each in one continuous length, housing 66 inmates. The plan is inflexible and there is a severe shortage of small-scale community spaces.

To complete the tally of the earlier new prisons is yet another type of design. This time it takes the form of a number of self enclosed courtyards, with strings of cells ranged along corridors.

This prison is at Muret and accommodates 610 inmates.

A more adventurous attitude towards prison design, freed from Ministry restrictions, is evident in the Maison d'Arrêt in Brest, the first built as part of a new programme. Its designer claims to take account of the psychological quality of inmate life, with a special emphasis on light and colour. There is, says the architect, 'a stark contrast between the exterior, which conveys harshness, and the interior which exudes the sense of an intensely vivid identity'. The exterior is certainly harsh and unyielding, with heavy concrete panels sloping inwards and upwards on one side in a rather menacing way. Nor can it be held that the interior appears much less intimidating, even with its much vaunted quality of light. But perhaps it is unfair to judge from photographs alone, without a visit. The main cell block slashes at an angle across the confines of the square walled perimeter in order to achieve a north-south axis. This allows east and west light to penetrate through the cells, spread with the aid of glass blocks set in concrete forming the inside walls. The prison holds 250 inmates, housed mainly in one long cell block split into groups of approximately 25. Cells face each other across a corridor, with fewer cells on the sloping side (which are wider but shorter) and a greater number of narrower, but longer cells opposite.

A different approach is found in the north of France where six new prisons are variations of a basic cruciform plan, adjusted according to site and local needs. Their sizes vary from 400 to 700 inmates, made up of men, women and youths, some awaiting trial as well as those sentenced. The cross-shaped plans either stand alone or are linked.

At the hubs are communal rooms serving small groups of prisoners. No corridors are more than five cells long in maximum four-storey-blocks. Modular units of 25, 100 and 200 can be created as needed, with varying degrees of independence. All the prisons are enclosed within a secure perimeter wall. Two principles have been applied in the design: ease of movement of prisoners to elsewhere in the prison, and the creation of a small-scale human environment to minimise tension and improve relations. These new prisons are thus very much in line with PDBS and New Generation thinking. Only the design is different.

Other small-scale prisons have been built in France under the Ministry of Justice programme 15.000. Designs vary from small star-shaped blocks of cells attached to the other prison facilities, to more traditional layouts with cells opening off corridors; all light years away from the enormity of Fleury Mérogis.

In addition, more campus-style institutions are being constructed. The Centre de detention at Mauzac in the Dordogne, for example, houses 240 male prisoners reaching the end of their sentences. The main aim is to help them develop individual responsibilities before release. The prison is in the shape of a village square surrounded by small residential buildings, within a secure perimeter fence. The living units house 12 men as small

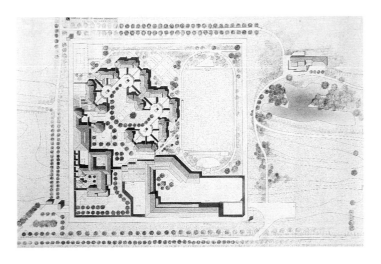

FROM ABOVE: *Fleury Mérogis, France, under construction (photograph: AVIA-TAXI); self-enclosed courtyard prison at Muret, France (photograph: YAN); smaller scale French prison at Mauzac, recently completed*

independent households. Although the barred windows give the game away, the buildings are as domestic as possible with pitched tile roofs.

New wine in old bottles

There is no country in the world which is not suffering from a surfeit of obsolete, overcrowded prison buildings. Conditions in many of them are vile and a disgrace to civilised society. To quote from just one prisoner on his experiences ' . . . hell on earth . . . a place that almost defies description . . . the building is damp . . . on entering the washroom one is overcome with the pungent smell of urine and faeces . . . there are two main landings with between 140 and 150 prisoners on each. There are just four toilets on each landing which are, more often than not, blocked and overflowing . . . showers are damp and crumbling, their walls covered in fungi. . .' This sort of letter (and far worse) can be repeated many thousands of times, if multiplied worldwide. Although 20 per cent of American prisons are less than five years old, a third are more than 50 years old. In the UK, there are 45 Victorian establishments; 18 built in the 1960s and 1970s; ten built in the 1980s; and a selection of 16 others of various types, prison camps etc. Even some of the more modern ones are showing signs of distress and may involve expensive repairs and refits. Their layouts are mainly of three types: radials (eg Pentonville); radials with separate accommodation blocks (eg Cardiff); separated accommodation blocks (eg Wormwood Scrubs, although the blocks have since been linked as part of an upgrading programme).

Other countries can produce a similar catalogue of unsuitable buildings, usually with open tiers of cells accessed by galleries, poor sanitation, and few of the extra facilities needed to run a modern prison. The solutions offered in the UK may serve to demonstrate how some of the problems can be overcome. The speeding up of the UK improvement programme became imperative after the 1990 riots, especially in providing more humane surroundings, and affording more control through the design of the buildings.

As mentioned earlier, integral sanitation for all cells (no more 'slopping out') will be completed by February 1996. This is being carried out in two phases: first, within larger contracts when prisons are upgraded; second, adding 16,500 toilet units to other cells. The total upgrading programme will provide also an additional 2,400 places by extensions and conversions in about 20 existing prisons. This is equivalent to between four and six new prisons. A great deal of other extra accommodation is being provided: better kitchens; workshops; recreational, administrative and visiting facilities; plus a range of other building works to make the prisons function more efficiently. Since the riots security and control have assumed even greater importance resulting in a number of constructional and operational changes:

– roof zones are better protected from illegal access by inmates.

Slates and tiles, which can be used as missiles, are being replaced by metal decking, steel mesh screens are being fitted below roof lights, eaves overhangs extended, and rainwater pipes protected to prevent climbing

– security of service ducts is upgraded; prisoners are zoned into smaller groups of up to about 60, by means of steel gates and grilles

– better locking systems are introduced

– cells are upgraded by fitting mesh and render to walls and ceilings, with washable durable finishes, floors are rescreeded, windows enlarged and fitted with high security steel grilles, cell doors strengthened and rooms rewired

– more efficient alarm systems are fitted

– external areas are zoned, with barrier supervision, and only one access into the prison is allowed from outside.

All these improvements need to be done in a way sympathetic to the architecture of the original, and in a holistic way as every change affects some other part of the prison, either in design or operational terms. English Heritage has issued guidelines for alterations to historic prison buildings. It has a number of particular concerns, notably changes in roofing materials, enlargement of windows in cell blocks, and emasculation of the simple massive nature of perimeter walls. Its guidance has not prevented arguments about enlarging cell windows, with its robust view that 'a prison should look like a prison . . . Prisons shouldn't look like warehouses converted into bijou flats'. It is at this meeting point of aesthetics and authenticity, with health and humanity, that most conflicts will arise.

However, both can be achieved with great success, as can be demonstrated by the rebuilt and enlarged Strangeways prison. This distinguished Grade 1 radial prison designed by Alfred Waterhouse in 1868, was badly damaged in the 1990 riot. It has been lovingly restored (but with additional security) and the cell wings vertically subdivided by steel grilles into smaller groups, without loss of character. Even the cell windows have been enlarged without harm to the original by lowering the sills. Large new additional facilities – an entry building, visitors' reception, food services, training workshops and physical recreation centre – have rescued a wreck and converted it into a fully equipped prison with many more years of future life. It is a model of what can be done.

A difficult and uncertain future

Legislators and prison administrators face a taxing future. After centuries of neglect and decades of experiment, there now seems to be more of a consensus that splitting prisoners into smaller groups in smaller buildings, with a more relaxed management style, may offer an answer. But there are lingering doubts in some quarters about whether New Generation really is the answer: some rigorous monitoring will have to be done. There is, too, a lack of clarity about what prisons are capable of achieving apart from containment. The view of Judge Tumim is that 'the future of prisons must lie in guiding the majority of prisoners. Prisons must help to reduce crime after release'. One way he believes this can be done is to introduce industrial prisons where paid work is at the core of the regime.

Perhaps the best, and realistically modest, hope is that by offering a range of work, educational programmes, recreation and discipline, some good may be done for some prisoners.

There is considerable alarm at the increasing number of people being sent to overcrowded prisons, and a belief on the part of reformers that prison is not the right answer for a large proportion of wrongdoers. But society at large is more vengeful and wants to lock up its malefactors in increasing numbers ('just deserts'), rather than dealing with them in other ways. In addition, types of crime and criminal are changing. The world is becoming more savage and dangerous; drugs are playing a worrying part in violent and apparently motiveless crimes; offences are being increasingly committed by very young adults and children; society is more fragile and the outlook more fearful to many people.

Depending on who is in power, political judgements will affect sentencing policy and have a profound effect on the use, numbers and types of institutions, and their regimes. It has been observed that 'you can't design the prison until you have designed the criminal justice system'. Where does this leave the architects and administrators who must grapple with the problems now? Most important of all, perhaps, is the amount of money available to be spent on prisons, as costs escalate and the market economy engulfs the justice system. Confinement costs are quite visible, but confinement benefits are more difficult to establish. The argument that providing more prisons would cost communities less than they now pay in social damages and prevention is probably specious, and depends on many factors including certainty of detection and conviction.

The old prisons will get older and even some of the newer ones are already showing signs of wear and obsolescence. More of those awaiting trial are now being held on remand. What are the implications for the prison building programme?

Privatisation will have a great impact on future prison design and management. For example, will income be related to the numbers of prisoners going through the doors or to a fixed fee from the government? Will the government be asked to provide some sort of guarantee that it will channel prisoners to the new privately funded and run prisons rather than to the Home Office run institutions? Prison staff may have to be convinced that under privatisation their role will be enhanced and safety guaranteed. Public accountability and protection of prisoners' rights must be paramount.

With these all-pervading pressures, a balance has somehow to be struck between, what Dr Sean McConville calls 'responsible humanity and irresponsible expediency'. That will be no mean task in the decades ahead.

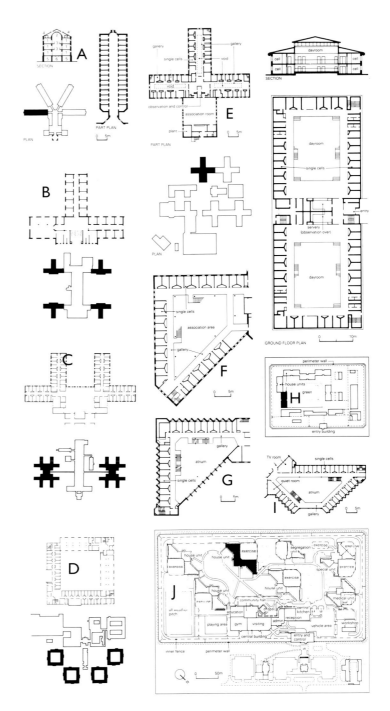

KEY TO PLANS: **A** *Typical radial prison (Pentonville, 1842);* **B** *Self-contained cell blocks (Blundeston, 1963);* **C** *'Telephone pole' prison (Featherstone, 1977);* **D** *Courtyard prison (Low Newton, 1978);* **E** *Galleried prison (Bullingdon, 1991);* **F, G, I** *'New generation' prisons (Doncaster, 1993; Milton Keynes, 1992; Lancaster Farms, 1993);* **H** *PDBS Prison layouts, 1992–;* **J** *Milton Keynes*

Prospectus

CEDRIC PRICE

A close friend described in the daily press a recent experience thus: 'At Tottenham Court Road police station I underwent police questioning. The hot and stuffy room that we sat in for nearly two hours was twice as tall as it was wide or long and a table stood between two policemen and myself. There were two doors to the room, one through which we had entered and the other, I imagine, led to the cells. High on one of its walls was a window that was made of glass bricks and which could not be opened.' As a result of this experience my friend, a peer, is going to oppose any move by the Government to do away with the Right of Silence.

This does at least show the positive constructive results of incarceration. More seriously, it indicates the enormous effect even such mild incarceration can have on future behaviour. Of course, if my friend had known the duration of the 'ordeal' at its commencement then I suggest the effect of such enclosure would have been considerably reduced.

To the architectural content of incarceration must be added an indefinite, or indefinable, time element to complete the condition. To be sentenced to a fixed term of detention in an 'open' prison scarcely constitutes incarceration, for the previously mentioned two elements are missing. It is difficult to 'imagine' an open prison with only windows of glass bricks, unopenable and beyond one's reach.

This introduces another element into the architectural vocabulary of incarceration – namely that of tactile and visual association through recall, or memory, on the part of the observer. Indeed, the role of the memory of association enables symbols of incarceration to be used to effect long after their reality is gone. The massively gloomy rusticated gateway to Stafford Gaol reminiscent of the main gate of old Newgate – long demolished, provides entrance to a run-of-the-mill nineteenth century prison, spacious and sanitary for the time. The idea of incarceration relieved only by death, achieved gruesome poetry by the last public hanging in the UK being held outside this very gateway.

Not far from Stafford, at Trentham, can be found the most sublime architectural expression of incarceration – the Sutherland Mausoleum – keeping the family secure and undisturbed for all time; unambiguous in comparison with Hawksmoor's mausoleum at Castle Howard. Incarceration can mean both imprisonment and confinement and it is in the full provision of the latter condition that architectural skills can be both observed and exercised to the full. Corbusier's La Tourette was originally designed for a Closed Order of monks.

Incarceration required by Closed Orders is achieved through architecture rendering the most populous and urban of sites wholly acceptable. The very same architectural elements and four-dimensional techniques employed actually or theatrically in the civil imprisonment can be employed by these Orders to help the inhabitants achieve the sublime oneness with God. The architecture of incarceration as an aid to Closed Orders is more likely to

be sensitive to the limits that the architectural contribution makes towards the achievement of this most rigorous of human control and patterning. The resultant architecture, through having to achieve the minimal intervention while creating the maximum degree of desired conditioning, is likely to be the most defined. After all, the users are voluntary and acutely demanding for the exclusion of the unnecessary. It is in this condition of desired incarceration that the most rigorous selection of both necessary and useful can be determined.

Society elsewhere has need of applied incarceration devoid of either social or religious appetites. Fever hospitals, nuclear laboratories, workshops in space, ice-cap submarines, atomic bomb shelters, sealed enclosed self-sustaining communities are some examples of enclosures in which people are voluntarily incarcerated for their own benefit.

Thus the question must be asked as to whether incarceration is for the benefit of those within or without. The silent accompanying question is, of course, 'for how long?'. These questions must be answered before an assessment of the architectural attention is required.

It is one of those questions which in its answer determines the difference between building and architecture and in so doing defines some of the unique qualities of the latter.

IAN RITCHIE

Confinement is, in the penal sense, a restriction of physical activity within a defined physical boundary. It has been, but should never have been a restriction on mental activity. From this it would follow that there are, perhaps, analogies with other institutions of confinement, such as schools (single sex boarding), monasteries and convents, perhaps even hospitals. Of course, incarceration is not a free choice, but historically in some cases, this has been true also for the aforementioned institutions. The evolution of prisons has recognised the fact that the imposition of physical hardship within the prison as a 'punishment', additional to the necessary confinement for public safety, is cruelty to the mind. Hence prison design, organisation and management has and ought to be increasingly focussed on curing the prisoner's mind, through understanding the origin and development of it.

All of our other 'institutions' are becoming more security conscious, although aiming to keep people out rather than in, yet when in, 24-hour surveillance is just as common as in prisons. Increasingly, parts of our city centres bristle with overt protection and surveillance equipment. It seems that our society is communicating a growing sense that we are physically untrustworthy. Our urban centres are becoming less places of learning, sharing and communication while the opposite, quite correctly, is becoming the intention of the prisons.

Perhaps because the nature of our 'free society' has lost much of its ability to provide a tolerant and caring environment, that to create such an environment within prisons will be an anathema to most people. Prison architecture is simply a physical manifestation of the predominant philosophy, which in turn is a reflection of what society considers to be acceptable retribution as interpreted by present government.

KISHO KUROKAWA

Bentham's panopticon, circular prison with cells designed around the central position of the guard should not be overlooked. This configuration, and exploitation of light, allow the guard to see the prisoner's silhouette clearly, effecting supervision of the whole. This formalising aspect is a typical example of ancient society's philosophy. Foucault denied philosophically this classic centrism in his Surveiller et Punir – Naissance de la Prison. Collapse of the centre engendered the shift from the age of centralised supervision to the age of supervision by individual centre. Current prisons, however, have not made progress from the nineteenth century.

Contemporary society has been changing from the industrialised society that was supported by modernism, to an information-oriented society. The ideal society of modernism aimed at a universal world that followed one sole world ideal and rule.

Prisons were sites for punishment. The basic spirit was one of retribution. In these facilities, the same pain was inflicted on the outlaws as they had inflicted on their victims.

The world of today has experienced transition from a society of universal rules to a society of symbiosis that recognises diverse cultures and diverse rules.

The industrialised society gave birth to Heidegger's concept of das Mann, the homogeneous, universal man. But in the informa-tion-oriented society, informational added value, or individuality and creativity, are the human raison d'etre. Especially in the field of art and culture, genius and creativity originate in the breaking of conventional rules, so that genius and lunacy differ only slightly.

If there are rules in such a symbiotic society which are common throughout the whole world, they might be only the rules: 'do not hurt or kill people' and 'do not deceive other people'. It will probably become necessary to observe the rules that are based on the cultures, religions, and systems of each country in working for the symbiosis of the world's cultures.

Prisons in the age of symbiosis must be like schools. The course of study should vary depending on the crime, and the period of education should also vary. Lifelong education may be necessary for those who commit serious crimes. The graduates must be returned to society, and the stigma of the prior conviction must be abolished.

If the prison is a school, it must possess a library, a lecture hall, and a movie theatre. Private study rooms, a language laboratory, vocational training rooms, a cafeteria, and a conversation lounge would also be useful.

Prisons hereafter should not be of the conventional design which facilitates observation by a guard: more open buildings should be used to allow for mutual exchange.

The walls or devices used to isolate the prison from society must be perfect. Still, since the prison itself is a city, its buildings should be made more open. Prison architecture should provide an appropriate environment to nurture the spirit of mutual respect for cultural differences and the world's various diverse values, mutual recognition of individuality, and mutual acceptance along with competitiveness.

A suffering minority group venting a longstanding grievance in an orderly manner (Leon Krier, 1985)

Federal Correctional Complex

Allenwood, Pennsylvania, USA

THE KLING-LINDQUIST PARTNERSHIP INC

his complex, the Federal Bureau of Prisons' largest completed construction project, indicates the shape of future prisons. It was completed in the spring of 1994.

Situated in the foothills of the northern Allegheny Mountains, three separate compounds house over 2,300 inmates: the Low Security Federal Correctional Institution (LSCI), medium security Federal Correctional Institution (FCI) and high security United States Penitentiary (USP). A Witness Security Unit (WITSEC) also operates as a separate facility for 54 inmates.

In response to the philosophy of the Bureau, the design seeks to provide an environment that is less institutional in character than traditional detention facilities. Thus, while based upon the dictates of security, it allows for interaction between inmates and staff and the encouragement of inmates in self-improvement through educational, vocational and social means.

The security requirements of the high security penitentiary are fundamentally different from the neighbouring complexes. Designed to accommodate 512 inmates, this compound is almost entirely internalised and isolated from contact with its surrounding environment. Inmate movement through the penitentiary is constantly and closely supervised by staff. Support functions, such as food service and gymnasium spaces, which normally attract large groups at the same time, are far separated to minimise concentrations of inmates in one spot.

The buildings of the USP form its inner security wall, the perimeter of which is completed by a continuous enclosed circulation corridor. The outer perimeter is secured by a double line of fencing with rolled barbed tape installed between the fences. A perimeter intrusion detection

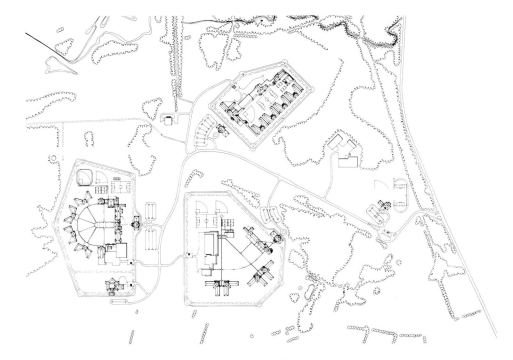

OPPOSITE: *Axonometric of housing unit with cells arranged around dayroom. (Photography: C Geoffrey Berken);* ABOVE: *Site plan showing the three compounds; USP is situated above and FCI and LSCI below, the main site entry from the highway is located to the right*

system is located at the inside fence and a road for patrol vehicles runs at the outside of the perimeter fence. Six guard towers, located near the corners of the security fence, maintain constant supervision over the facility and surrounding site.

Each of the four housing units integral with the perimeter wall, is composed of two storeys with 16 cells per floor arranged around two sides of the central dayroom. The third dayroom wall, lined with recreational and counselling spaces on the first level and mechanical spaces above, effectively isolates the units from views to the surrounding site. An open officer's station centrally located within the dayroom is positioned for direct supervision of the programme spaces, the unit sally port entry, and the doors of the inmate cells.

Arranged radially around the western edge of the courtyard, the entries of the four housing units of the medium security compound, FCI, focus to the centre of the space, effectively minimising hidden corners. The triangular shapes of the housing units promote the Bureau's desire for increased interaction between inmates and staff. An elevated officer's station near the entry to the dayroom affords maximum visual supervision of cells, corridors,

OPPOSITE: *FCI plan with WITSEC unit to the left – 1 outside administration; 2 inside administration; 3 inmate systems; 4 health service; 5 special housing; 6 gymnasium; 7 passive recreation; 8 education; 9 religious and assembly; 10 vocational training; 11 personal services; 12 food services; 13 general housing; 14 maintenance; 15 UNICOR; 16 vehicular sallyport*

OPPOSITE BELOW: *LSCI plan – 1 outside administration; 2 inside administration; 3 inmate systems; 4 health service; 5 special housing; 6 gymnasium; 7 passive recreation; 8 education; 9 religious and assembly; 10 vocational training; 11 personal services; 12 food services; 13 general housing; 14 maintenance; 15 UNICOR; 16 vehicular sallyport*

ABOVE: *USP plan – 1 outside administration; 2 inside administration; 3 inmate systems; 4 health service; 5 special housing; 6 gymnasium; 7 passive recreation; 8 education; 9 religious and assembly; 10 personal services; 11 food services; 12 general housing; 13 maintenance; 14 UNICOR; 15 vehicular sallyport; BELOW: USP courtyard*

dayrooms and support spaces. This
solution requires less staff with no reduc-
tion in control.

The campus type layout of the low
security institution, LSCI, reflects the
relative freedom of inmates within.
Security is provided by the perimeter
fence, detection system and armoured
patrol vehicles. Each of the four housing
units can accommodate up to 248 inmates
in dormitory-style cubicles rather than
cells. This arrangement promotes interaction between inmates and staff, while
allowing effective supervisory control of
the unit.

The units are arranged in two wings of
62 cubicles, each joined by central offices
for the unit manager and staff, and a large
multi-purpose room for inmate use.
Support and smaller social spaces are
grouped around the open officer's station
for casual but frequent supervision. Equally
important to the design, which seeks to
encourage reasonable social behaviour, is
the need for a secure unit that is simple
and inexpensive to build, and adaptable to
varying site and environmental conditions.

Design guidelines and codes set by the
Bureau were consulted for Allenwood,
covering all aspects in detail, from security
fencing and spatial layouts, to the furnishings of cells and the use of light colours.
Cafeteria furniture is bolted to the floor to
prevent it being lifted up and thrown.

The architecture of Allenwood's main
facilities reflects the character of vernacular residential buildings native to the
region. Building forms wherever possible
are highly modelled and reflective of
function, reducing the scale of individual
facilities. Predominant are low one- and
two-storey structures of masonry and glass
with dark sloping metal roofs which echo
the contours and colours of the mountains.

The masterplan is designed to maintain
existing vegetation both for the sake of
preservation and for visual buffering of the
facilities from surrounding roads and
communities. Supplementary plantings of
trees consistent in type with those of the
region line the primary access road
through the site and provide additional
buffering of the facilities where necessary.

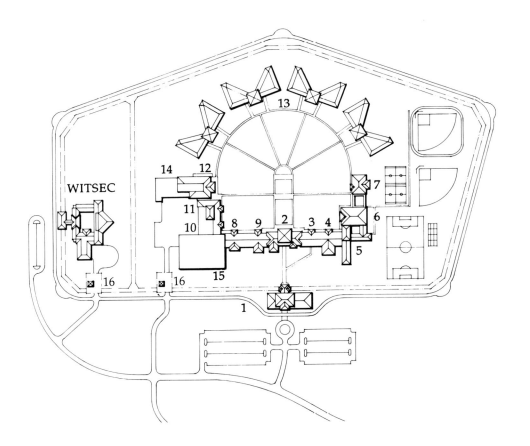

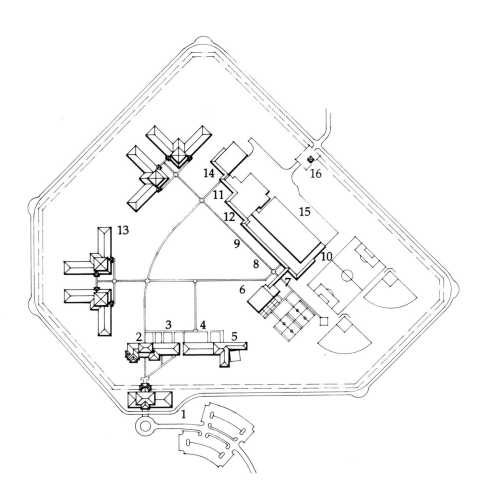

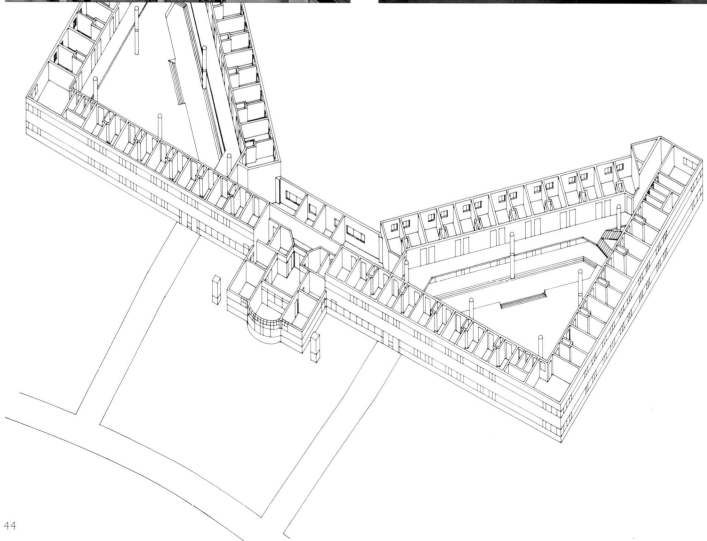

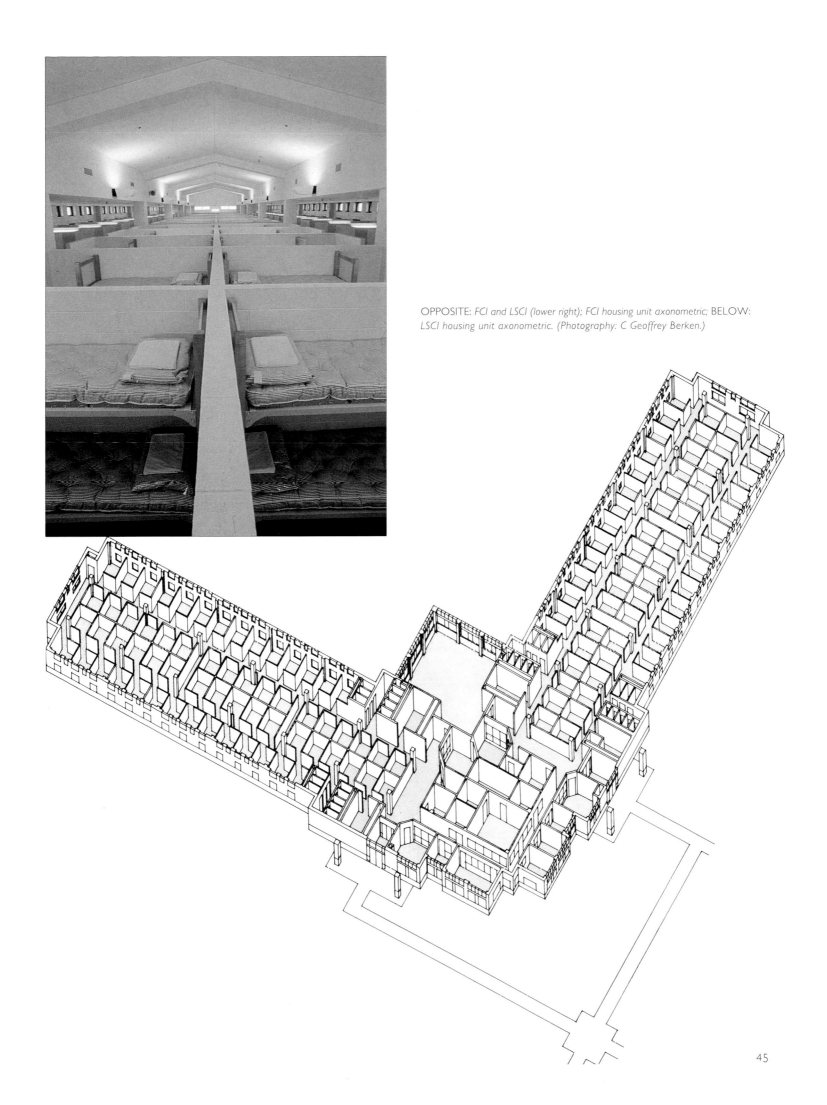

OPPOSITE: *FCI and LSCI (lower right); FCI housing unit axonometric;* BELOW: *LSCI housing unit axonometric. (Photography: C Geoffrey Berken.)*

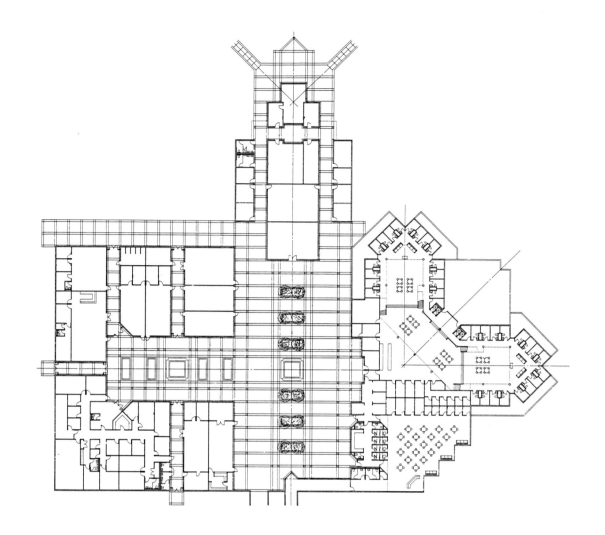

West County Justice Center
Contra Costa, California, USA

DWORSKY/DESIGN PARTNERSHIP

This podular, medium-security facility is set in 50 acres, located between a major regional park and a municipal golf course. Completed in 1991, it was designed to supplement Martinez Detention Facility, the first direct supervision facility built in the USA ten years earlier.

The campus-like facility is intended to create as normal an environment as possible, with a strong focus on remedial education. Low-rise buildings which are unlocked during the day accommodate 560 inmates who are free to move unescorted throughout the campus for programmes and activities, reducing staffing requirements. The buildings of the podular facility

are arranged around a central quadrangle where educational, medical, religious and visiting functions are linked via an open-air gabled arcade.

Outside the security perimeter are located operations such as administration, inmate booking, food preparation and laundry services. The perimeter is guarded by a motion detector, an infrared security system and a patrol road. The high-level security perimeter allows more conventional construction methods to be used inside, such as laminated dry-wall construction with a plastic finish coat between each cell and the dayroom, wooden doors, and more normal furnishings.

The housing units contain 64 'dry' cells

which have access to clustered toilet facilities. A sliding door between the paired units allows operation of two units by one officer during the night. The design enables the officer to see and hear clearly what is going on throughout the unit.

A relaxed and calming environment is created by the architecture which reduces the risk of violent activity and vandalism. This enables such facilities to be constructed in a more cost-effective manner.

OPPOSITE, FROM ABOVE: *Lower level plan of facilities inside security perimeter; section looking south through multi-purpose room; elevation looking south; elevation looking west; BELOW: Site plan*

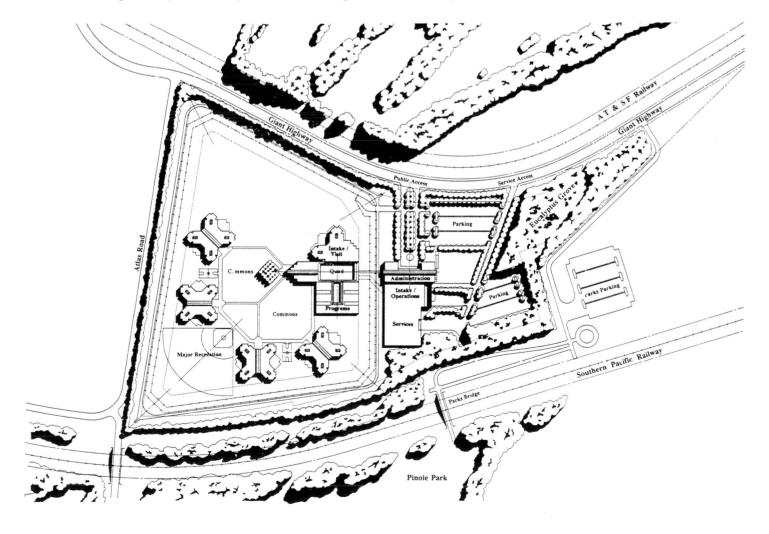

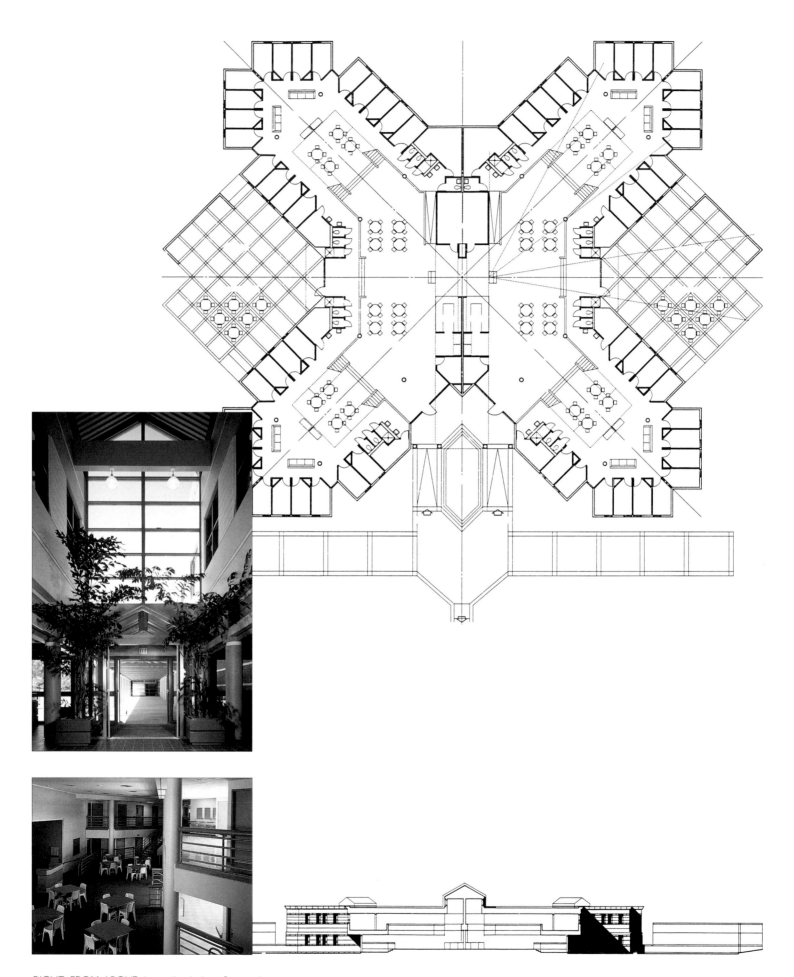

RIGHT, FROM ABOVE: *Lower level plan of general population housing; section through dayroom*

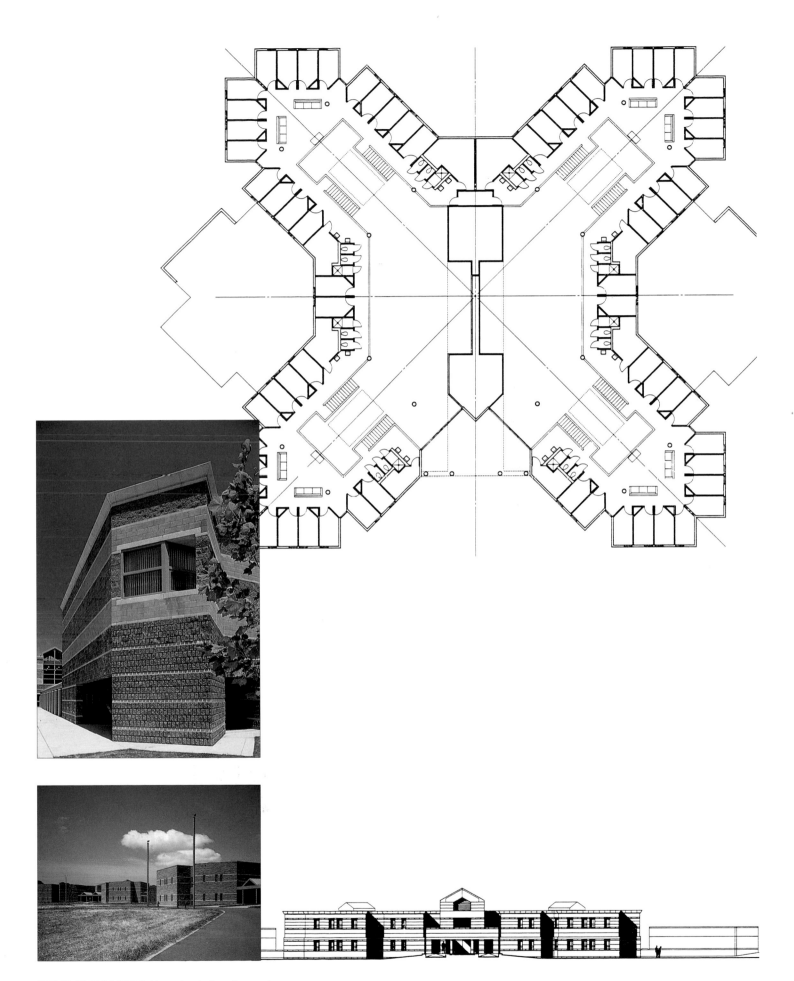

RIGHT, FROM ABOVE: *Upper level plan of general population housing; elevation of entrance facade*

Sheriff's Operations Center and Jail Complex
San Joaquin, California, USA

DWORSKY/DESIGN PARTNERSHIP

This integrated and consolidated facility brings together all the County Sheriff's personnel and operations contiguous to a new main jail complex, complete with medical, mental health and dental facilities. The facility was constructed after the West County Justice Center, Contra Costa and provides 1,280 beds for pre-trial housing on a 150-acre site west of Stockton, California. It has been well organised for immediate needs and accommodation of future growth.

General population housing is arranged in two 512-bed compounds. Separate housing exists for intake classification, medical and segregated populations. Each of the direct supervision housing units has 'dry' sleeping rooms with free access to toilets and showers. The dayroom is positioned to afford good visual control over the pod for the floor officer and immediate access to all service areas.

Ample natural light and a variety of activity spaces are provided by the housing unit design, which also takes into consideration the monotony of dayroom activities by opening up interesting and varied spaces. The sweeping curves of the exterior and use of both subtle and warmer tones throughout the complex, create a more pleasant environment for staff, inmates and visitors.

OPPOSITE: *Model of site (photography: Adrian Velicescu; centre left: John Sutton); FROM ABOVE: Site plan; axonometric of main building with sheriff's operations/jail core. Located to the right are medical and intake housing*

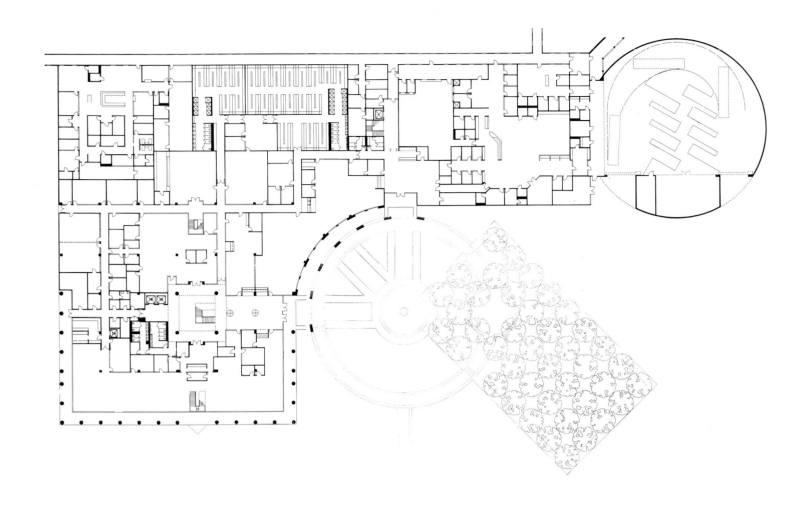

FROM ABOVE: *Ground floor plan of sheriff's operations/jail core, with vehicle sallyport on the right; section through core looking north; south elevation and section; west elevation;* OVERLEAF: *Ground floor plan of general population housing; section through segregation and general population housing looking north. (Photography: John Sutton.);* PAGE 55: *Axonometric of housing compound; section through compound looking north*

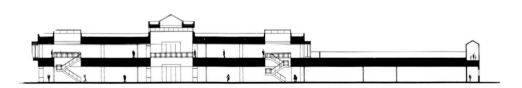

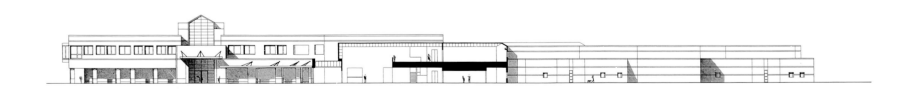

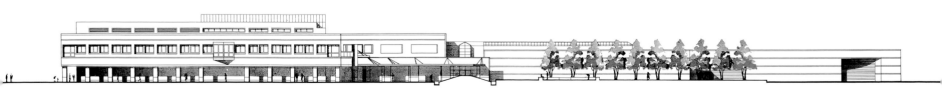

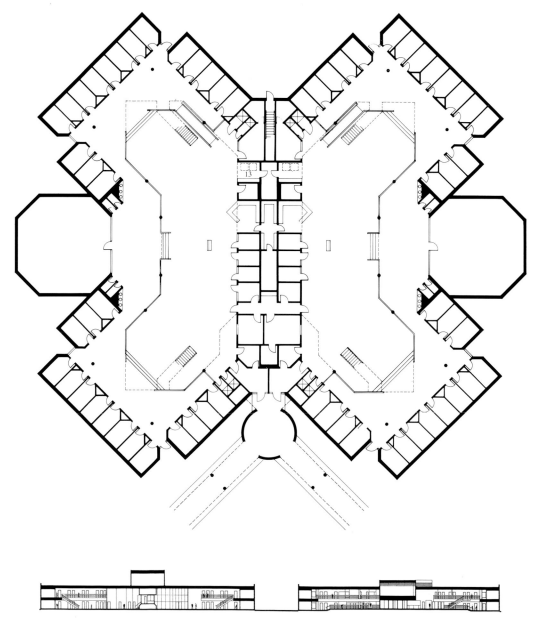

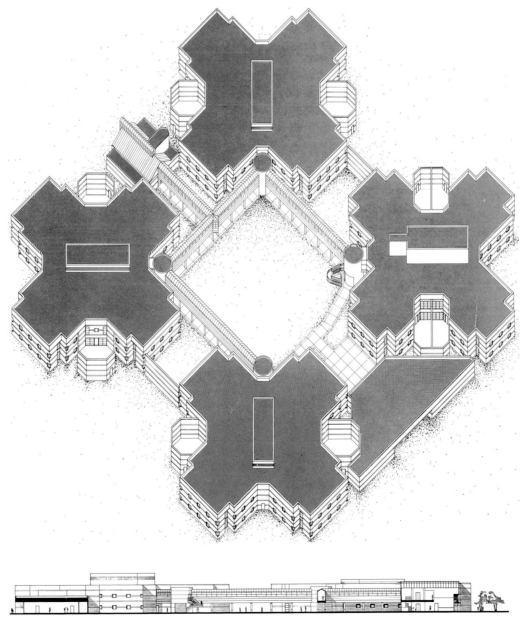

Leon County Detention Facility
Tallahassee, Florida, USA

RICHARD D NELSON COMPANY/HANSON LIND MAYER

Leon County, in response to current and future detention needs, set out to expand its correctional system by renovating 300 existing dormitory beds; converting its existing jail into a Sheriff/Law Enforcement Center, and building a replacement Detention Facility.

The Detention Facility, completed in 1993, consists of 776 beds with core support facilities to accommodate future expansion for a total of 1,444 beds. The facility houses male and female pre-trial, pre-sentenced, sentenced, and juvenile offenders.

Direct supervision unit management housing clusters enable inmate movement to be minimised in an environment that enhances access to programmes and services. Each cluster provides direct access to an activity centre with space for counselling, education and exercise.

The design also allows for an increase in bed capacity through double-bunking, without additional expansion to the centralised management core. Visitors travel directly to housing units via a walkway on the mezzanine level, and a secure service corridor separates access and view of all services from inmates and visitors.

The remodelling of the existing jail into the new Sheriff's Department/Law Enforcement Center provides a smooth transition with minimum interruption to the operation of the facility during construction. The Center's location outside the secure envelope of the detention complex, allows existing services and parking areas to be utilised by both facilities.

RIGHT, FROM ABOVE: *North, south and east elevations. (Photography: George Cott.)*

Bartholomew County Jail
Columbus, Indiana, USA

HISAKA & ASSOCIATES / SILVER & ZISKIND

Columbus prides itself on being a small city with the greatest concentration of exemplary modern buildings in America, selected by a private foundation. This building, completed in 1990, is the 60th to be added to its list of important projects.

The challenge in designing a building of this nature was to contribute positively to the existing context as well as establishing a civic identity for the building itself. It lies on a principal entry to the town, close to the County Courthouse, and includes two distinctive structures: a linear, rectanglular building fronting Second Street, housing the County Sheriff's department and public space; and a 16-sided irregular polygon housing a 116-bed maximum security facility. These are connected by a bridging tower containing stairs and elevators.

Placement of the public functions in the linear building fronting Second Street facilitates a public interface, belying the stigma often attached to a jail. The public entrance opens into a two-storey lobby. Articulated portals lead to ground floor offices and monumental stairs allow access to an interior balcony, inmate visiting, and the offices of the Sheriff and his staff.

The form of the drum is generated through functional considerations: the radial plan facilitates ease of operation with inmates' cells ringing the perimeter on the second and third levels. These open on to a double-height communal dayroom lit naturally by clerestory windows. Removed from the street and capped by an open-air steel cage housing the secure outdoor inmate recreational area, its form reinterprets that of the traditional dome and provides a memorable civic image.

Patterning of warm brick, splitface, and precast trim breaks down the scale of the elevations in a manner reminiscent of the character of the town's older buildings.

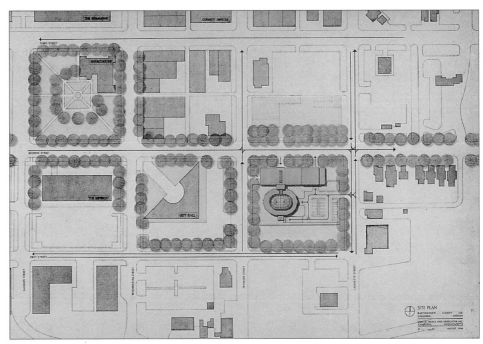

ABOVE: *Site plan*; PAGE 61, FROM ABOVE: *Second level plan; ground level plan; north-south section.* *(Photography: Balthazar Korab.)*

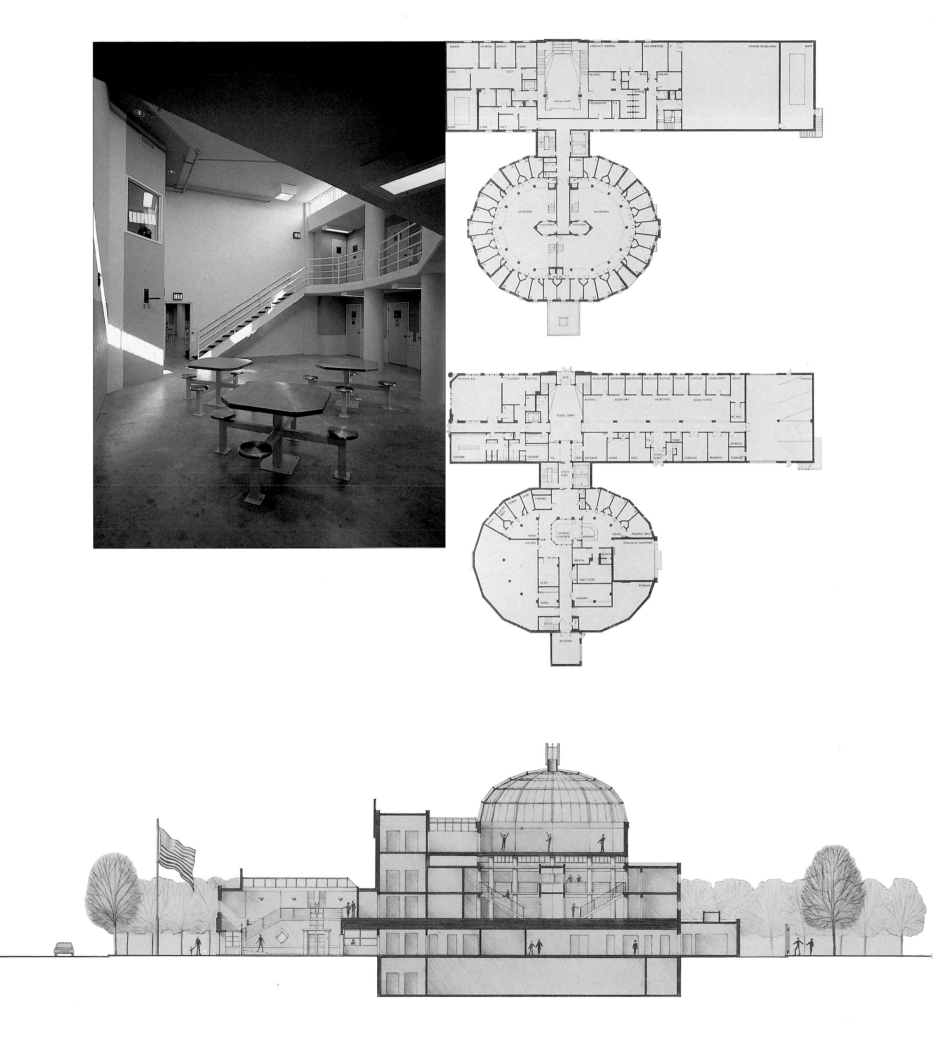

Federal Correction Institution
Marianna, Florida, USA
RICHARD D NELSON COMPANY/HANSEN LIND MEYER

This multi-security-level correctional complex accommodates 1,304 inmates in an environment designed to be as normal as possible, facilitating interaction and communication between the inmates and staff. It was completed in 1988.

The unit management approach is adopted to provide casual observation of inmates during daily activity hours by non-supervisory staff. Extensive educational and federal UNICOR industry (furniture manufacturing) programmes help to promote inmate self-improvement skills in a structured environment.

The main 550-cell medium security correctional institution for men is designed with all the components necessary to establish a self-supporting community. (Double-bunk capacity is 1,100 beds.) This includes housing, administration, education, recreation, medical clinic, food service and dining, vocational training and industrial warehouses.

Freestanding within the complex is a 54-bed facility for the maximum security female population, separated from the main compound by internal security fencing. This autonomous unit is equipped with its own security control, programme and service areas.

Adjacent to this main institution is a self-contained 150-bed minimum security camp for female inmates nearing release. A central utility plant services the entire complex.

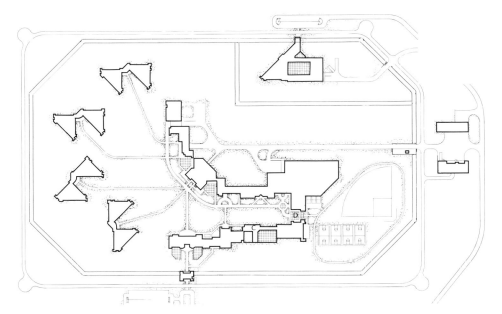

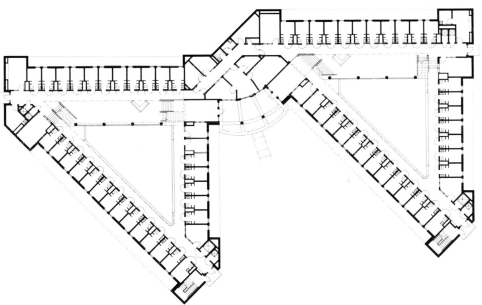

FROM ABOVE: Site plan showing witness security facility (above), inmate housing units (left), multi-use, educational and food services (centre), reception, administration and health services (below), warehouse and energy plant (right); inmate housing unit plan. (Photography: Phil Eschbach.)

Main elevation of Administration

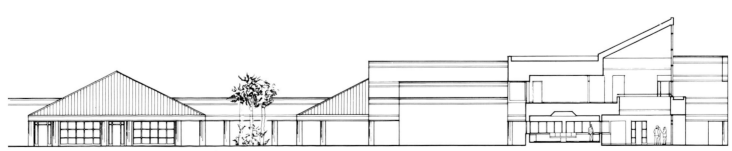

Section through Administration

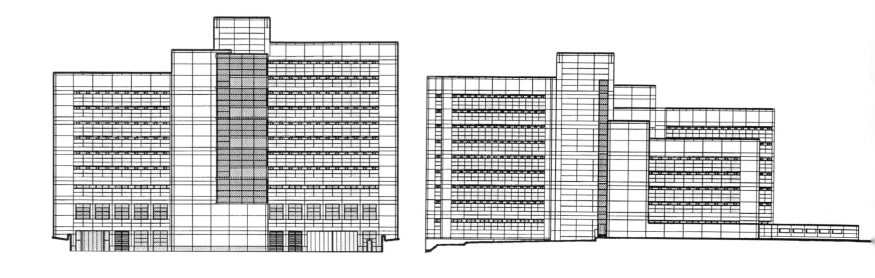

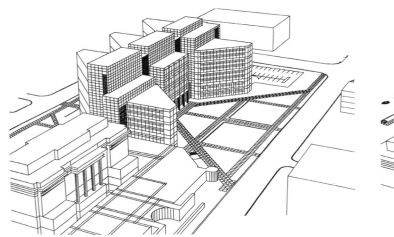
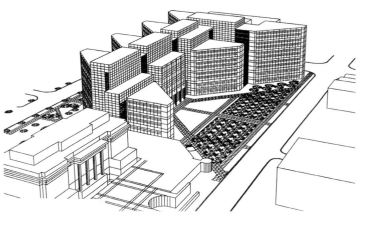

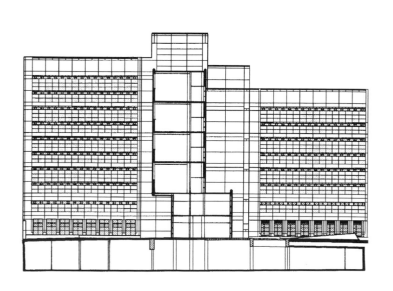
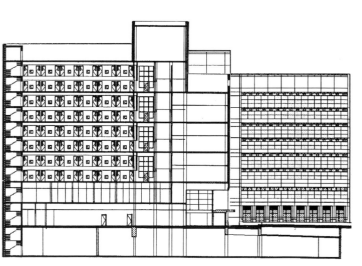

Intake and Detention Facility

Mecklenburg County, Charlotte, North Carolina, USA

LITTLE/HELLMUTH, OBATA & KASSABAUM

This project involves designing a pair of urban intake and detention facilities within an existing government complex. Along Fourth Street, the existing raised forecourt of the courthouse is completed and contained and a new public plaza created, aligned with the existing plaza across the street.

A less tense atmosphere is provided by open-plan processing areas with colour coded, airport-style seating zones; the assumption being that arrestees are co-operative and are treated respectfully (though back-up security is always close at hand). Flexible waiting areas are arranged to allow pre-trial interviews to occur before or after magistrate hearings and booking. Magistrate hearing areas are elevated to maintain their importance in the hierarchy of spaces. A separate reception desk and public service windows give concerned members of the public access to court services and on-line information on the status of an arrestee.

In the podular housing areas, direct supervision and 'dry' cells help to foster a normal environment, while saving money by eliminating remote controlled security hardware, security doors, plumbing fixtures and special chases. Inmates have keys to their own cells. The triangular forms of the housing pods and the horizontal glazing bands relate to the nearby government office building. The tall, sheer facade to McDowell Street provides the interface for future expansion and creates an urban edge marking the entry to the Government Center. The building mass steps down to the plaza and towards the western end in deference to the old courthouse. Facades are of precast concrete, coloured and textured to relate to the site's older limestone buildings and articulated to give a restrained modern expression appropriate to the nature of the project.

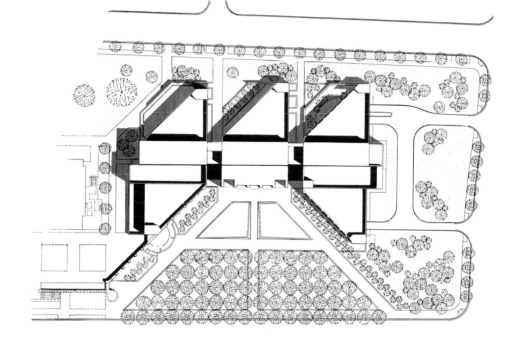

OPPOSITE, FROM ABOVE L TO R: *East elevation; west elevation; phase I; phase II; sections;* ABOVE: *Site plan – services and vehicular access is on the right, off South McDowell Street, with the possibility of future expansion; the new public plaza is created in front of the jail's main entrance along East Fourth Street, located below*

USPHS, Federal Correctional Complex

Florence, Colorado, USA

LESCHER AND MAHONEY/LKA PARTNERS

The USPHS, (United States Penitentiary High Security) was completed in July 1993. It is part of a masterplan for the location of four prisons and penitentiaries of varying degrees of security, as well as accompanying support facilities.

In a site of 49 acres the facility includes areas for administration, health services, and educational programmes, as well as a chapel, gymnasium, commissary, laundry and barbershop. These are located opposite the inmate housing pods arranged around the recreation yard. Of the total number of 586 beds, approximately 15 per cent are special housing units.

The USPHS uses the direct supervision method of management with a state-of-the-art, electronic security system; control activities are administered at one station. Additional security is provided by a perimeter fence, seven guard towers and a patrol road. The building wall itself also acts as a security line for no inmate cell window looks outside the exterior building line. All external recreational facilities and circulation for inmates are contained within the building perimeter.

The Bureau of Prisons and the design team set out to establish an environment that both acknowledges the nature of the maximum security programme while being of humanist origin. The building forms are sheathed in a field of dark red brick with buff-coloured horizontal striping. An intentional balance exists between respecting the architectural heritage found in the area and investing the building with an identity of its own that is appropriate to the complex.

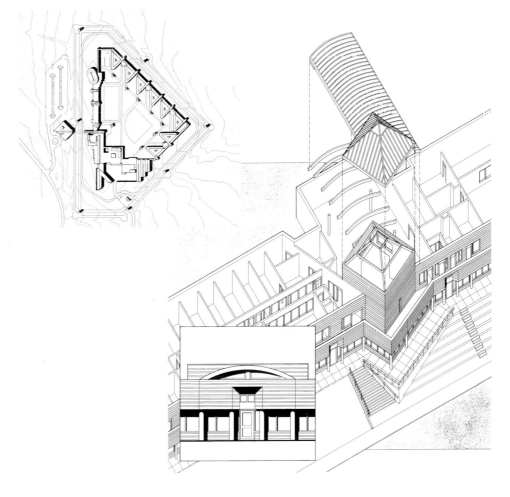

RIGHT: *Site plan, with administration building on far left, and vehicular sallyport below; exploded axonometric of core building and elevation detail*

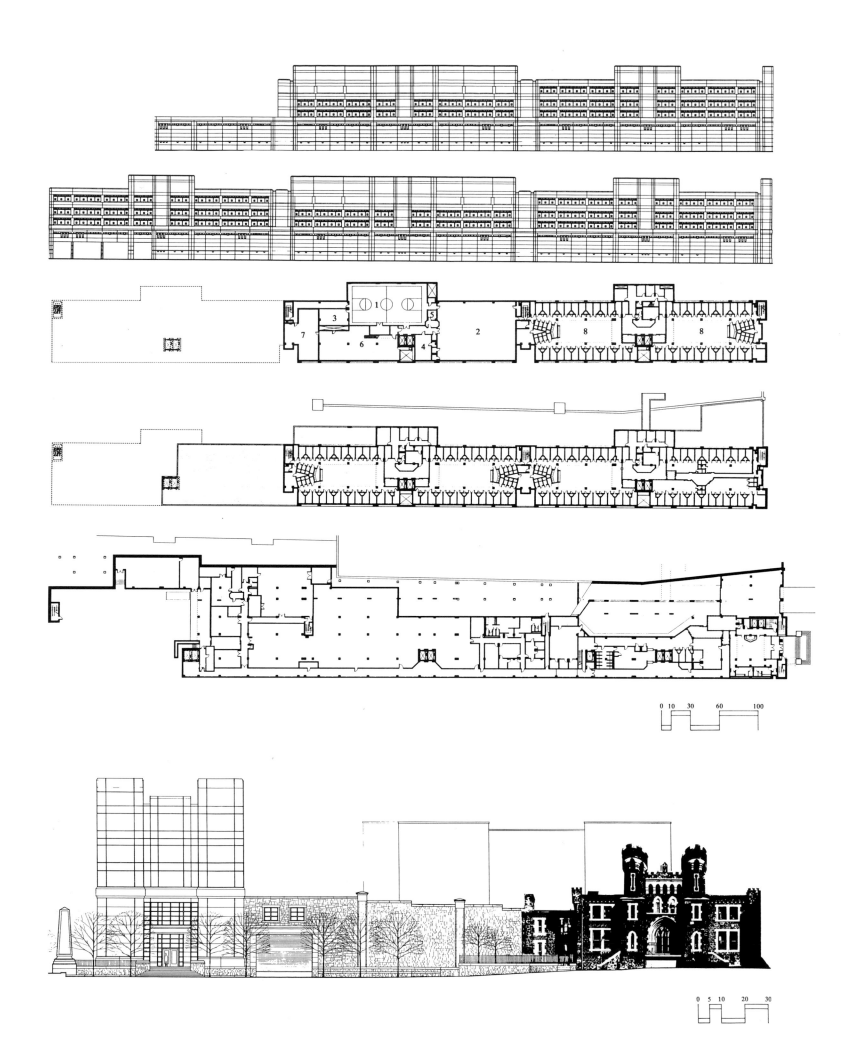

Central Intake and Booking Facility
Baltimore, Maryland, USA

SMEALLIE, ORRICK AND JANKA/HELLMUTH, OBATA AND KASSABAUM JOINT VENTURE

 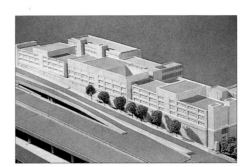

This 279,206-gross-square-foot facility is scheduled to open in 1995. It is designed to fit a narrow, sloping tract of land located between the nineteenth-century Gothic-style building of the State Penitentiary and a freeway. Within its walls the booking operations, currently taking place in nine police districts throughout the City of Baltimore, will be consolidated into a centralised unit.

More than 800 inmates will be housed in the third to fifth floors, in 50-person podular units with direct supervision management. Recreation, interview, exam and multi-purpose space will be located there to reduce the movement of inmates. An indoor and outdoor basketball court and exercise room will be on the fifth floor.

The second floor will accommodate legal services, interrogation areas, holding cells, and an infirmary. On the first floor, newly arrested individuals will be taken through the booking process. Inmate movement will be monitored by bracelets with bar codes. Information kept by a variety of law-enforcement agencies will be centralised and immediately accessible.

This facility will greatly increase efficiency and expedite the processing of arrestees through the location of Court Commissioners, Pre-trial Services, Public Defenders and State Attorneys. Photographs will be taken by computer, as will fingerprints which will be matched against unsolved case files. The offenders will not even have to be transferred to court for bail hearings: it will come to them via video teleconference.

The urban jail features a cast-in-place concrete structure and a facade consisting mainly of light-grey precast concrete panels. The oppressive effect of bars is avoided by utilising a combination of porthole and thin ribbon windows.

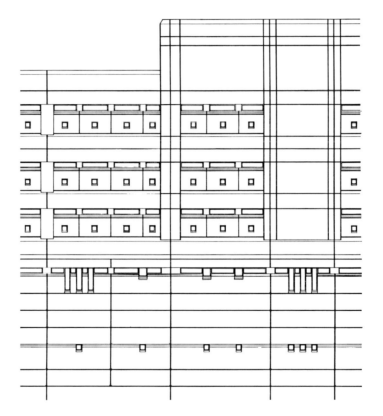 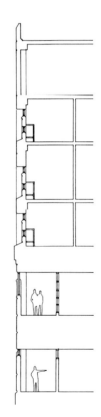

OPPOSITE, FROM ABOVE: *West elevation, for 500 beds; west elevation for 750 beds; fifth floor plan; third and fourth floor plans, indicating future expansion on the left; first floor plan; south elevation showing the existing monument on the left and historic administration building on the right;* ABOVE: *West elevation/section*

73

Dare County Jail
Manteo, North Carolina, USA

L ROBERT KIMBALL & ASSOCIATES

Dare County Jail was designed to accommodate an ultimate capacity of 200 inmates with a first phase construction capacity of 120 beds. The building was completed in 1992 and houses pre-trial, short term, sentenced, maximum custody and sentenced work release inmates.

Management of the facility combines centralised and decentralised functions. A central location for the facility administrator provides overall management. Within the housing units, the inmates are managed by decentralised control at the housing unit level. Although some of the inmate programmes and activities are centralised, most occur at the housing units where inmates dine and visit.

Those who participate in education, religious services or other programmes do so in a central location. Use of the centralised programme areas is scheduled to allow all housing units access, while keeping certain populations separate, including female inmates and special management inmates.

Externally, the simple contour of the building volume is accentuated by the use of blue colour. This is also applied to interior furnishings and structural components. Glass is treated in a constructive and original way which, combined with blue detailing, serves to create an unusual and interesting facade.

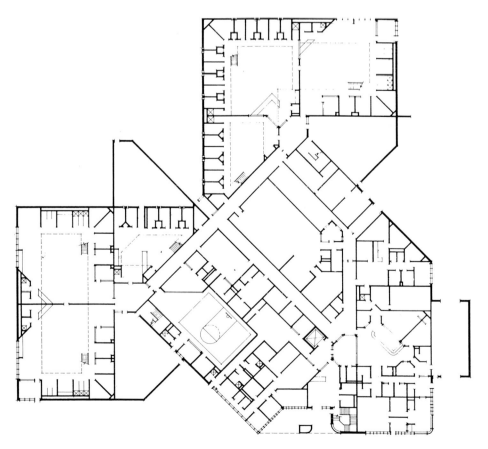

RIGHT: *First floor plan with booking and intake area to the right; administration, food, educational and recreational facilities are in the centre, leading into pre-maximum custody, pre-trial and sentenced work release (above). To the left of the plan are the women's unit, short term intake, and sentenced county/state. The triangular areas indicate outdoor recreation space*

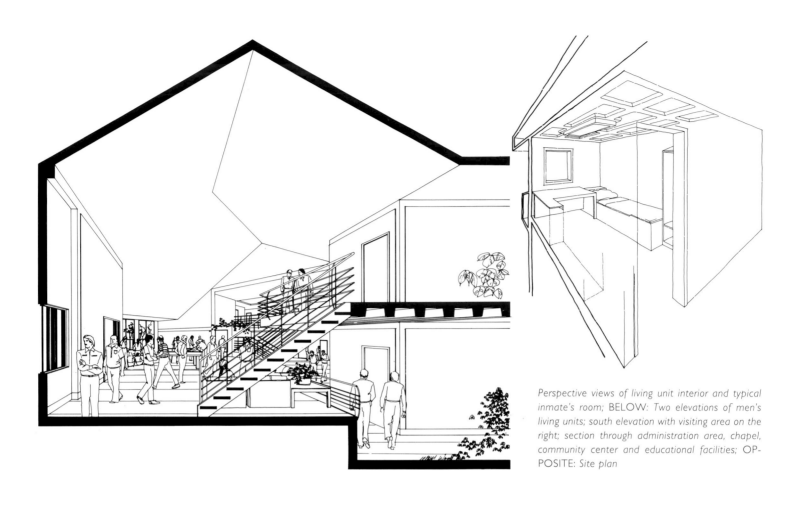

Perspective views of living unit interior and typical inmate's room; BELOW: Two elevations of men's living units; south elevation with visiting area on the right; section through administration area, chapel, community center and educational facilities; OPPOSITE: Site plan

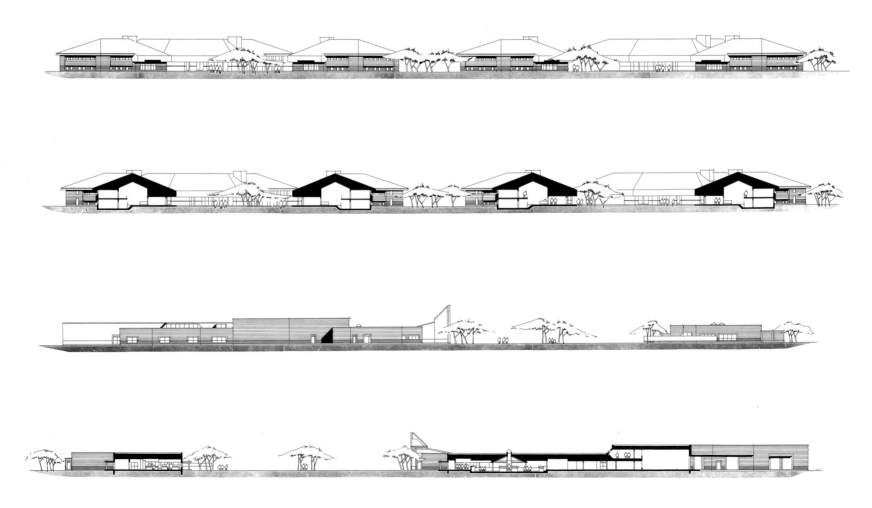

Fort Saskatchewan Correctional Centre

Alberta, Canada

WOOD GARDENER O'NEILL O'NEILL ARCHITECTS

This medium security complex, completed in 1988, replaces the old Fort Saskatchewan Gaol which became obsolete as a facility to effectively accommodate inmates of a special classification and provide programmes essential for correction and rehabilitation. The site is located in an area south of two highways, within city boundaries. Trees and berms effectively screen the Centre from view.

The complex houses both male and female inmates and officers; viewed by psychologists as a positive rehabilitation step. The design responds to this with a secure setting that is as normal as possible. A campus-style facility consisting of ten discrete buildings is contained within a security fence supporting a sophisticated electronic control system. This innovative freestanding, precast concrete antigrapple security fence has a smooth curved top cap and an architectural finish, using exposed aggregate and light sandblasting.

Single room accommodation is provided in buildings of residential character; each with pitched roof, large overhang and brick finish. Interior spaces are enhanced by abundance of natural lighting, bright colours and graphic treatment. The walls of the living units are precast concrete and the upper level floors are cast-in-place concrete. Thus intermediate floors are supported without erecting interior columns, providing an unobstructed view of the unit interior. Split level design incorporates common areas and staff facilities at the intermediate grade level. The unit officer is located in an open area by the main entrance, from where he can monitor the electronic security and life safety systems and be afforded survillance.

The unit clusters' arrangement allows for future expansion. Segregation of the facility encourages inmates to participate in such daily activities as going outside to another building and engaging in activities within different settings, as if in any normal community. A large area inside the Centre is for visits: a key factor in the rehabilitation process and preparation for release. At the hub of the campus is the open central dining area and adjoining circulation spaces in the Central Activities Building.

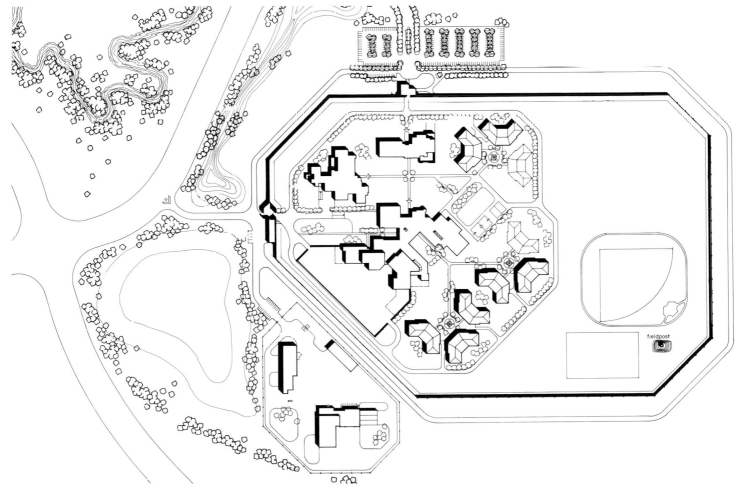

Living units perspective

Central Activities Building perspective

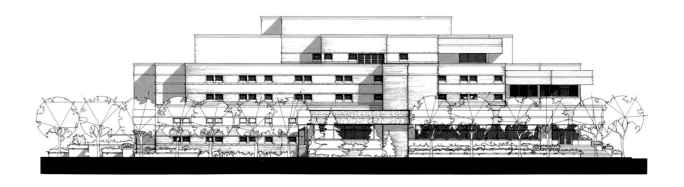

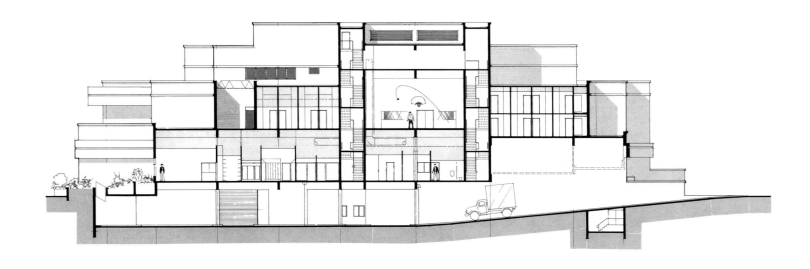

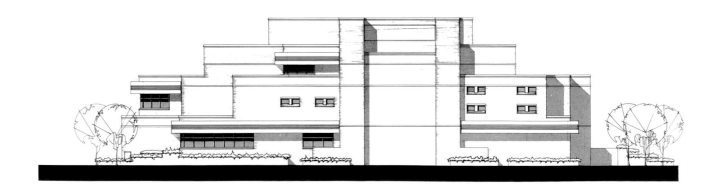

Red Deer Remand Centre
Red Deer, Alberta, Canada

BARR RYDER ARCHITECTS & PLANNERS

This remand centre, completed in 1986, is located to the east of the major downtown core of Red Deer. A distinctive civic architecture provides facilities for male and female offenders, including minimum security, remand, segregation and detention as well as a unit for young offenders.

Distinct operational zones related to the respective functions were thus required. Horizontal separation occurs between minimum security on the main level and medium/maximum security units on the second level. These units use the indirect method of supervision, enclosing the officer within a control booth. The combined Young Offender/Future Adult Remand Unit is located on the third level and employs the direct supervision method of management.

As each of the subsequent levels is smaller in area, the distinction of pro-gramme types by security requirements also allows for significant terracing, effectively reducing the overall building scale. The facility design was developed to optimise the efficiency of each level. A central circulation spine, linked to a secure elevator core connects the diverse functions and provides the clear circulation desired.

Massing, building height and material allow the Centre to blend with the adjacent courthouse, to which it is con-nected by underground tunnel, and the neighbouring buildings. In response, the major element of facade treatment is brick, which also provides the opportunity to articulate the building form.

Horizontal detailing and pre-finished aluminium louvred canopies reduce the scale of the building, effecting a stronger horizontal impact while protecting entries from weather and shading the south and west glazing. Cell windows are detailed to appear larger and de-emphasise the bars.

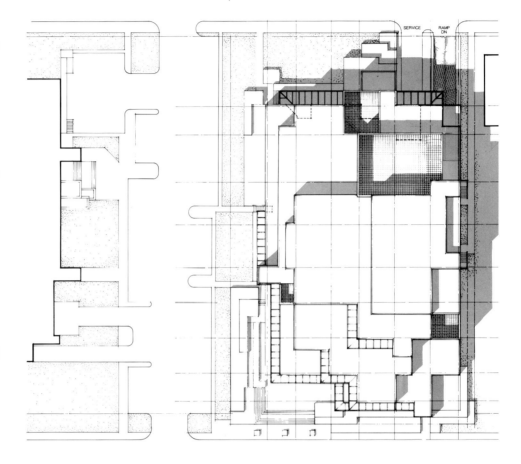

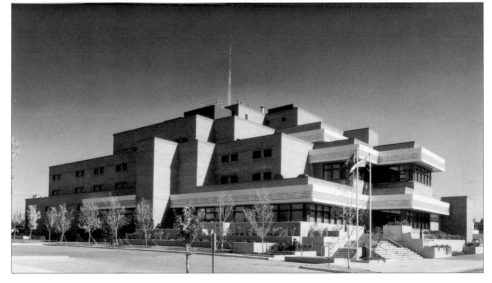

OPPOSITE, FROM ABOVE: *West elevation; section; east elevation;* ABOVE: *Site plan*

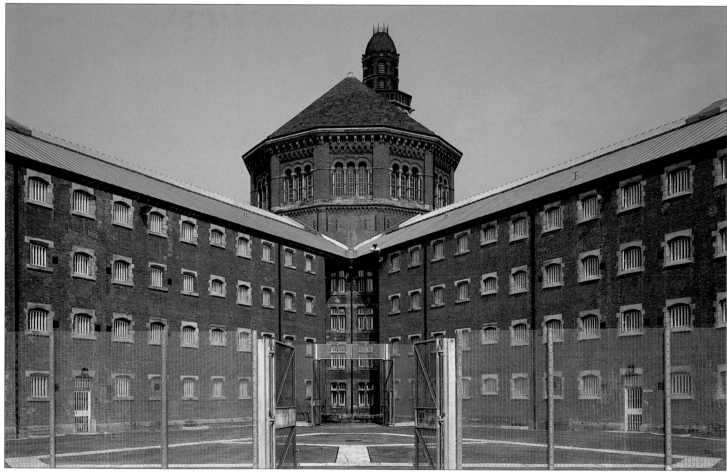

HM Prison Manchester (Strangeways)
Manchester, UK

RESTORATION AND ADDITIONS BY JOHN R HARRIS PARTNERSHIP / AUSTIN-SMITH LORD / JOHN BRUNTON PARTNERSHIP

Built in 1868 to the design of Alfred Waterhouse, Strangeways is a carefully detailed brick and tile prison in the Victorian Gothic style.

The building is radial in shape with six wings of cells, four storeys high, emanating from a central rotunda. Later additions include a smaller radial remand prison (not designed by Waterhouse) plus a clutter of other buildings.

After the 1990 riots, the Home Office decided to repair and refurbish the main cell blocks, provide a new entry building with offices and visiting rooms along the main frontage, and develop workshops, a kitchen and physical recreation centre on a site to the north, linked to the main prison compound by a bridge over the intervening street. The opportunity was also taken to clear the site of some of the later excrescences.

The main prison interior was subdivided vertically by open steel grilles, roughly half way along each cell block, thus creating smaller groups of prisoners. Further improvements in safety and security were also undertaken, and integral sanitation and larger windows were provided in each cell.

The masterplan for the whole site and the rehabilitation of the cell blocks were undertaken by John R Harris Partnership. Austin-Smith Lord was responsible for the entry building, and John Brunton Partnership designed the sports halls, workshops and kitchen. *Leslie Fairweather*

Photographs this page and overleaf right courtesy of the Home Office; all others © Chris Gascoigne

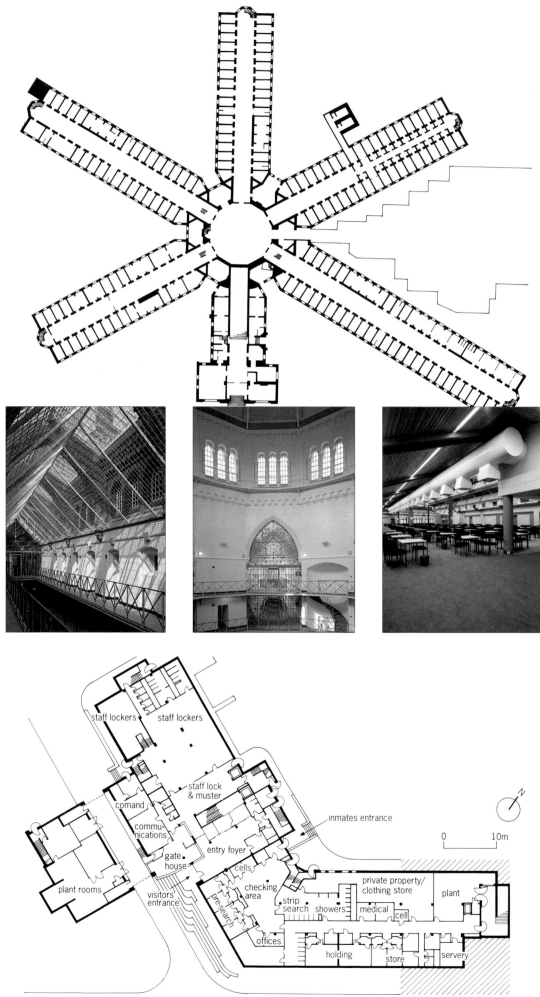

ABOVE AND BELOW: *Plan of main building before reconstruction; ground floor plan of entry building*

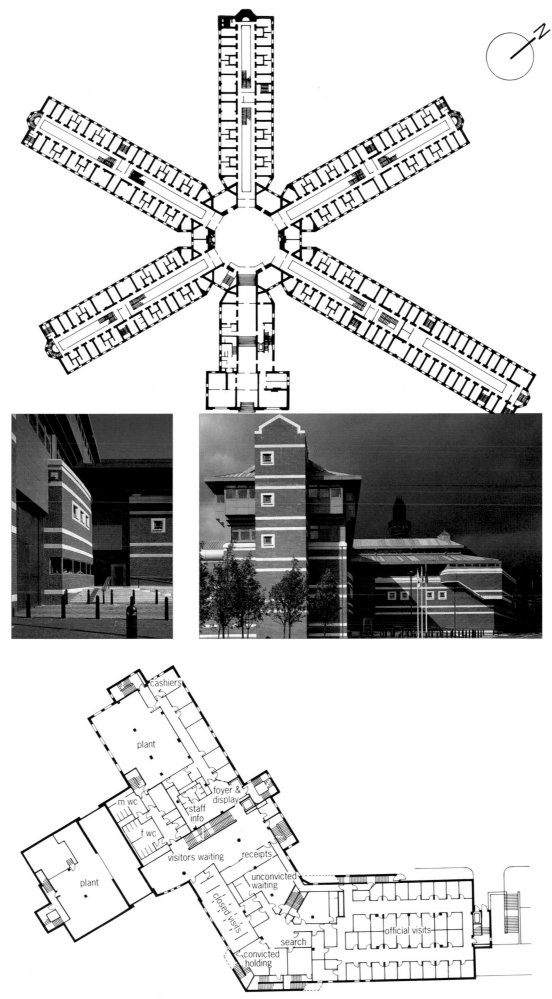

ABOVE AND BELOW: *Plan of main building after reconstruction; first floor plan of entry building*

HM Prison Doncaster
Doncaster, Yorkshire, UK

TBV CONSULT / J SEIFERT

The design of Doncaster Prison, completed in 1994, follows key recommendations of the Home Office and PSA Services Working Party's 1984 examination of USA developments in the design of prisons. The Home Office stipulated in its brief that the prison should be local to court facilities; requiring special facilities to allow for the high number of visits inmates on remand are entitled to receive.

In the manner of the American federal prisons visited, two-storey house units were developed around a multi-use dayroom, triangular in plan form and accommodation. These were divided into two units of 60 inmates to facilitate control and interaction in a less institutional environment. However, this would not provide the brief's requirement of 720 inmate places and led to the first steps towards the development of 'multi-storey' house unit designs in the UK, connected by a spine. Long columnar windows to the house units provide natural light to the association and recreation areas behind, while preserving the unity of elevational form and detail.

A 'T'-shaped amenity block, the hub of the complex, incorporates and links by a series of top-lit atria, the chapels, library and educational facilities, shop and an observation and assessment unit. Other buildings provide for medical needs, visits, physical recreation, reception/discharge offices, kitchen, stores and ground maintenance; outside the perimeter are a staff social centre, visitors' reception centre, works services unit and car parks.

The building and linking secure corridors create a series of courtyard spaces. Columns supporting the secure corridor provide rhythm and give a sense of scale to the overall development.   *Andreas Alexiou*

FROM ABOVE: *Site plan; triangular house unit plan; section through multi-storey house unit showing central spine. (Photography: Robert Wilkinson.)*

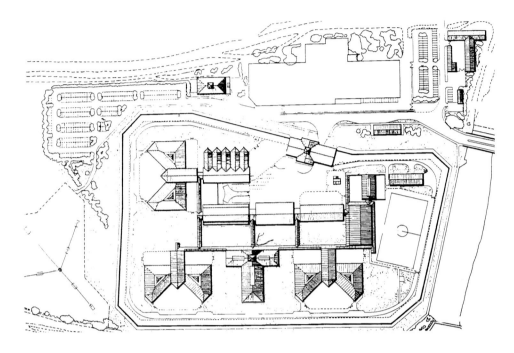

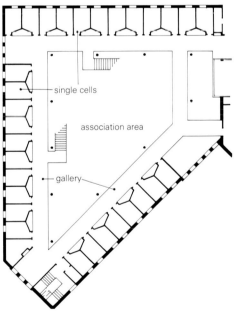

single cells

association area

gallery

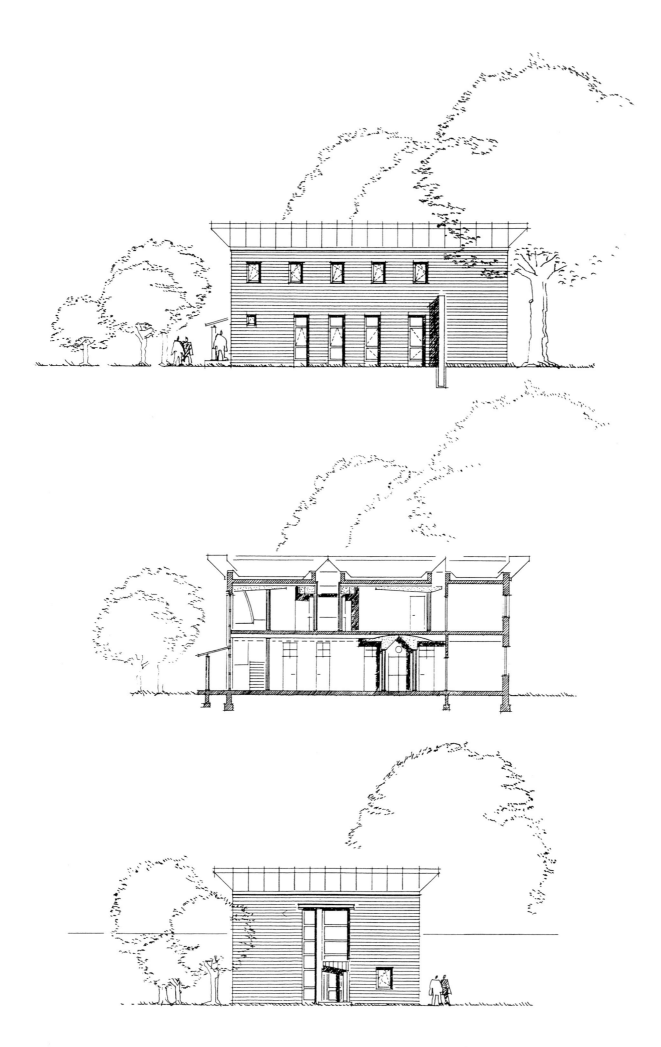

Mutter-Kind-Heim, Justizvollzugsanstalt III
Frankfurt am Main, Preungesheim, Germany

ROLF GRUBER

This award-winning mother and child home was completed in 1988. It stemmed from an instinctive reaction not to separate newborn babies from their convicted mothers. Research into children's behaviour when separated, indicated a lag in important developmental stages. However, when 'imprisoned' with their mothers, the children's development was seen to remain uncurbed in this respect.

The mother and child facility, which is part of a correctional facility for women, incorporates baby rooms and nursing care for the children, while providing places for teenage/adult mothers to develop their social skills.

Designing a prison to accommodate innocent children poses an interesting brief and encourages sensitive treatment of the living environment. First floor windows exist with a view to the outer world, yet cannot be opened for security reasons. Ventilation is facilitated by mechanical means. Ground floor columns help to reduce the feeling of being locked in.

Throughout the building, subtle use of materials can be discerned; taking care at the same time not to provide hiding places. This is coupled with a pleasant range of colours, such as yellow, pink and a variety of pastel shades. Decorative treatment of this nature is also applied to the exterior's blue-green striped roof which helps to mask security features.

The Mutter-Kind-Heim succeeds in providing a secure and constructive carceral environment for mothers that does not inhibit the life of their children.

OPPOSITE: *West elevation; cross section; front elevation;* FROM ABOVE: *Ground floor plan; exploded cutaway isometric and axonometrics. (The adjacent correctional facility is illustrated on page 91.)*

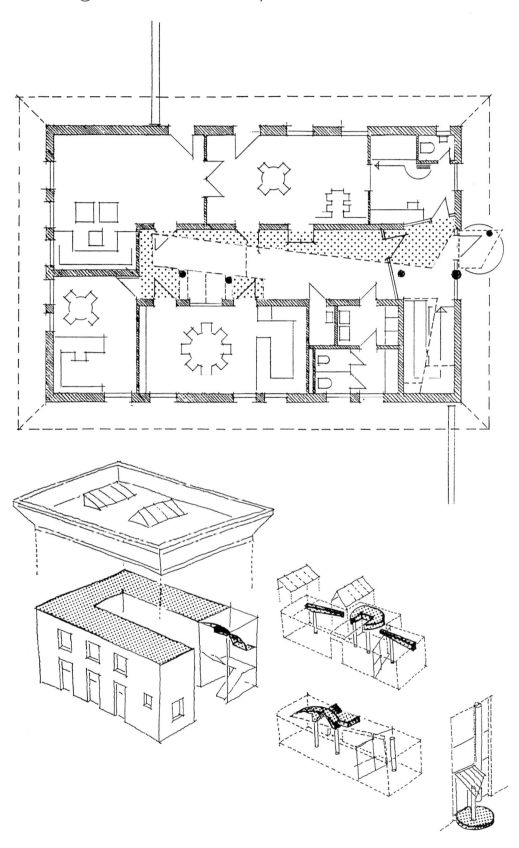

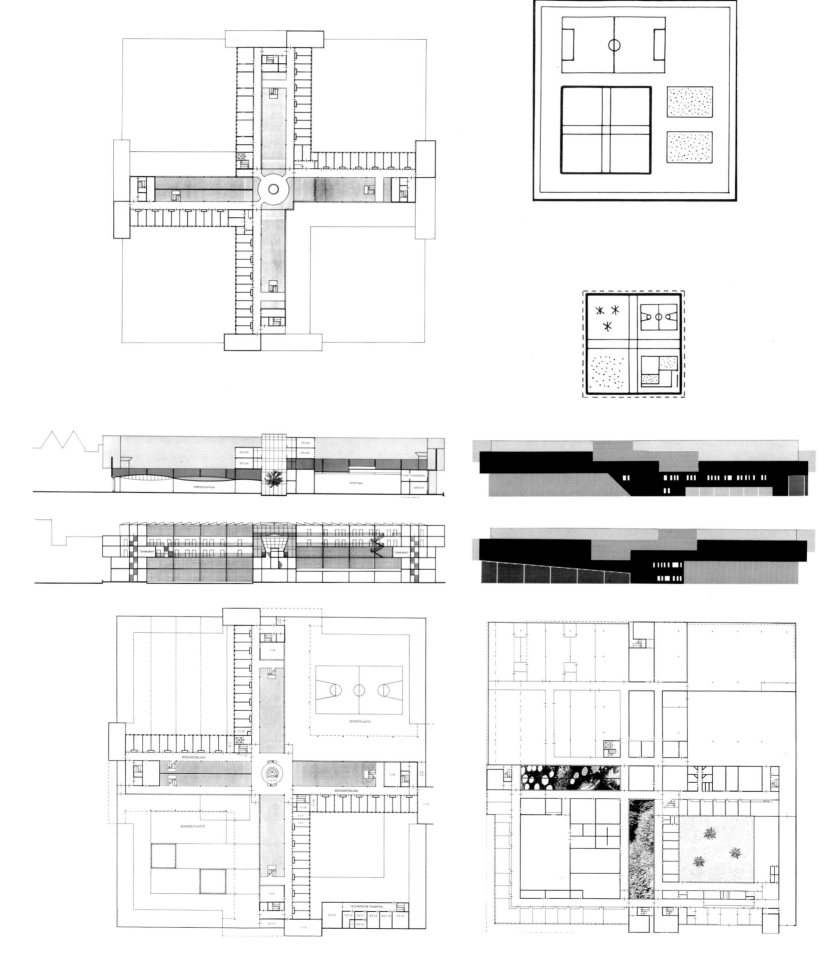

Typology Study
The Netherlands

WILLEM JAN NEUTELINGS

By the end of the century the Dutch Government intends to construct 5,000 new prison cells. The implementation of this task is hindered by the current shortage of suitable sites within The Netherlands. Following an international competition in 1993, Neutelings was commissioned by the Dutch State Building Department to investigate a new prison typology and is currently developing a new compact, low-rise prison that can be located successfully in both a rural and urban context.

In the traditional prison, the perimeter wall is at least 15 metres from the building. Sports fields and walking areas are located on the ground, producing a building complex that covers a surface area of at least 2.5 hectares. With sports/walking areas proposed for the roof, prisoners no longer access the external ground surface. Therefore, it is possible to change the edge conditions of the building while maintaining security specifications; reducing the surface area of the building to 0.8 hectares. This enables the number of potential sites, especially in difficult areas, to be increased.

The systematic diagram (*see right*) shows a composition wherein basic quadrants are manipulated to form a flexible design element offering a wide range of different prison solutions, specific to size, organisation, route and spatiality. Four quadrants are connected by a cross of atriums. When the cells (a) are on the exterior perimeter of the quadrant, the panopticon type is formed with an inner courtyard area (B); when placed on the internal side, the cruciform arrangement is formed with galleries within the atrium (A). Furthermore, the quadrants can also be filled with an activity centre (d), service centre (g), administration (i), labour (h) or transport court (j); allowing the roof to be used for sports fields or walking areas.

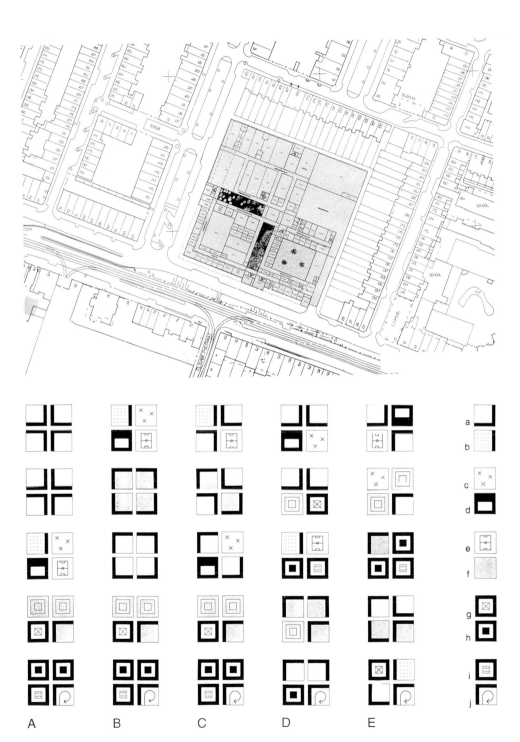

OPPOSITE, FROM ABOVE L TO R: *Roof plan; transition from traditional type to more compact model; sections and elevations; second floor plan; ground floor plan;* FROM ABOVE: *Compact model located in typical nineteenth-century urban fabric; systematic diagram*

De Geerhorst Penitentiary
Sittard, The Netherlands

SWINKELS/PASSCHIER/BONNEUR/WESTLAKEN

Aslightly sloping site facilitated the incorporation of different levels in the design of De Geerhorst Penitentiary, evident in the entrance and inner courtyards. In addition, an almost perfect square form gave rise to the idea of a fairly centralised arrangement for the complex, which was completed in 1989.

Four courtyards facilitate smaller groups and a greater diversity of utilisation. The inner courtyards double as recreation grounds; the two courtyards adjacent to the recreation wing contain a small football pitch and volleyball/basketball field.

Careful arrangement of building elements help to decrease staff numbers. The security lodge is situated at the centre of the intersecting wings of cell blocks. Each wing contains two groups of 12 cells, at the end of which are located a communal living room for the inmates and bathroom facilities.

The 252 cells are built in two and three layers around an open space with a glass roof. The cell blocks' staircases lead to the inmates' corridor benneath and to the four courtyards created by the intersecting wings. This corridor gives access to the recreation, service and workshop buildings; medical and visitor facilities are in the service building.

The gatehouse (see *opposite*) with security and access control facilities is located in the opening in the encircling wall. From the first level, ramps lead into the centre of the complex giving access to peripheral buildings and workshops.

Architectural features at Sittard are intimately related to the building's structural principles; the steel frame being visible to a greater or lesser extent, emphasising the utilitarian nature of the design. The colour white is predominant throughout the complex, and the site's natural characteristics are made use of to visually open up the prison complex.

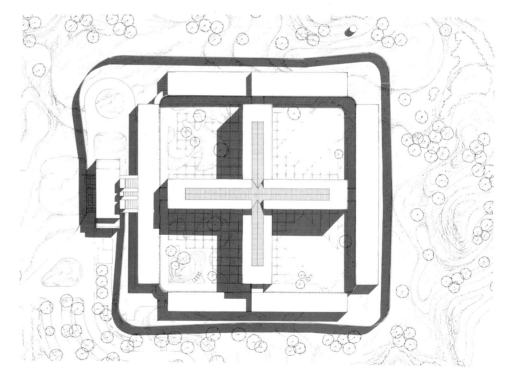

Site plan: the brief specified a double barrier; prisoners trying to escape would have to cross at least two security 'rings'. A five-metre-high wall surrounds the entire prison, within which there is a circle of buildings six-metres high. The cell blocks are located along the cruciform, inside the inner ring

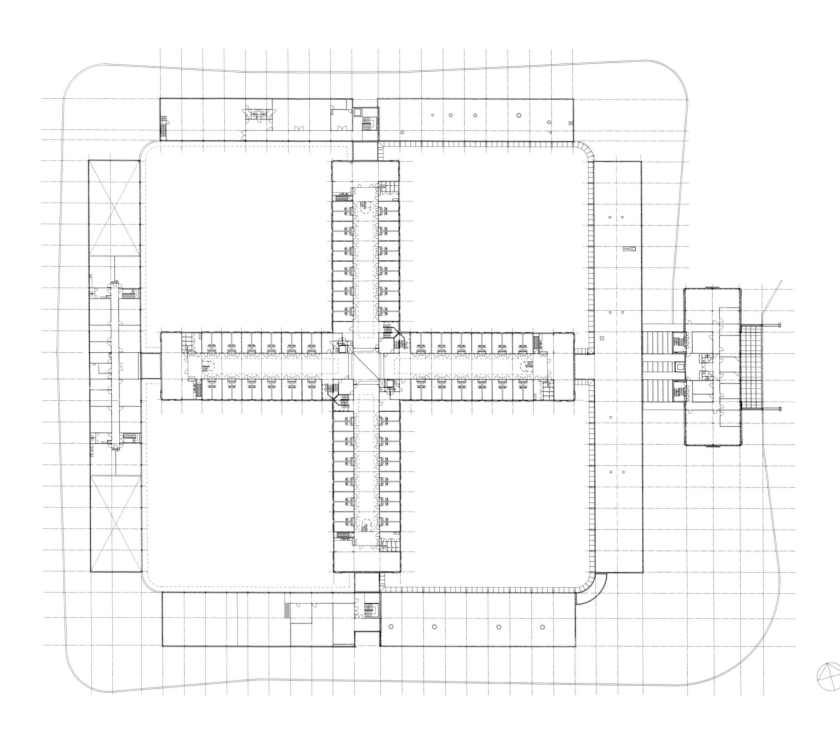

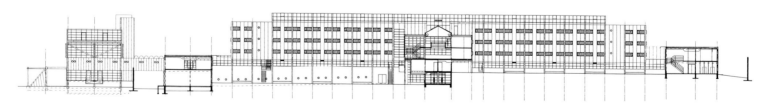

FROM ABOVE: *Third floor plan; sections*

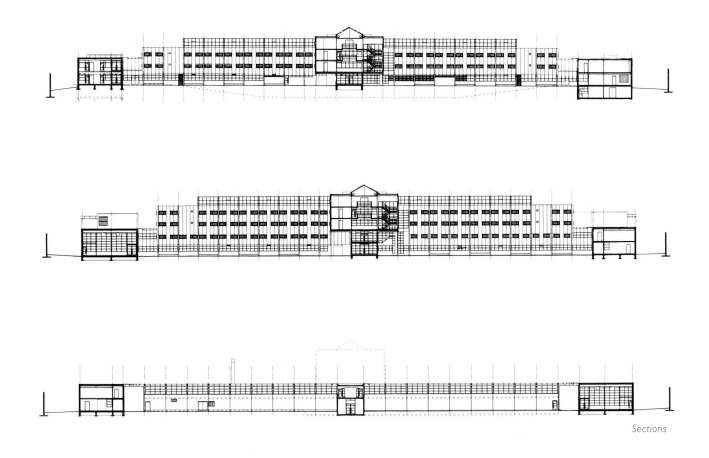

Sections

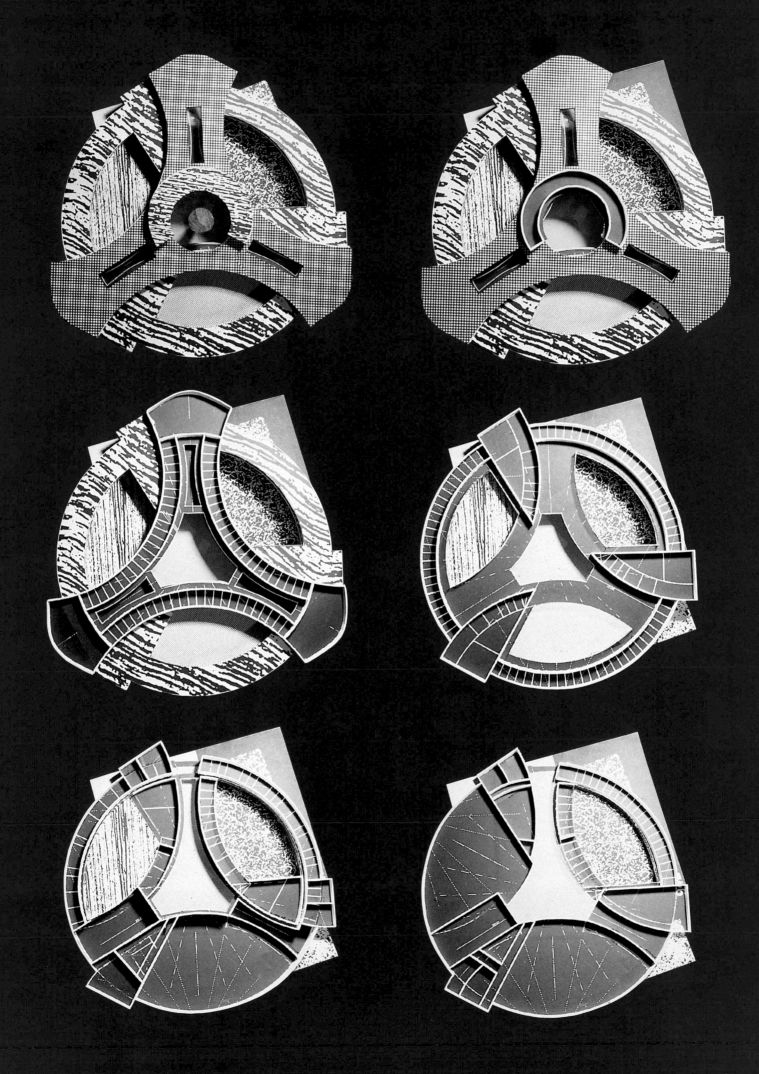

Typology Study
The Netherlands

KEES CHRISTIAANSE, GERARD VAN HOORN AND TICHO SAARISTE

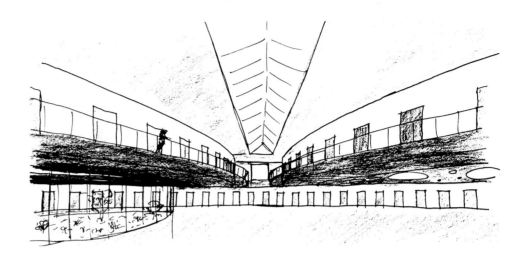

This programmes returns to the old archetypal prison design: the panopticon principle; facilitating a direct view between the guard's monitoring room and the cell doors.

Several types of penitentiaries can be distinguished in The Netherlands since the nineteenth century, relating to the social and cultural climate of the time in which they were erected: the prison with a dome-shaped roof and cells encircling a central point, providing a panoramic view for the guard; the pavilion complex with spacious layout, in housing groups of delinquents, sometimes together with the guards (presumed to have a therapeutic effect); the electronically monitored penitentiary, often of larger, more complicated structure requiring camera surveillance.

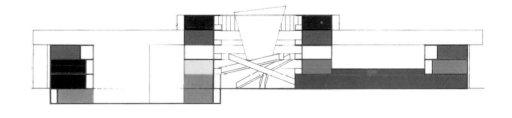

This is an exploratory study of how to design a compact, architecturally interesting and liveable building on the basis of new, more severe regulations. For safety reasons this Spartan programme falls back on the old panopticon principle, the most common examples of which are the ring-, cross-, or star-shaped prison buildings. By superimposing the ring-principle and the star-principle for the organisation of the cells, a three-dimensional ensemble comes into being that preserves the panopticon idea. Between the ring and the star segments, patios are formed which can be used to draw daylight into the underlying spaces, or as airing space for prisoners. The segments of ring and star have an identical radius and can use prefabricated construction.

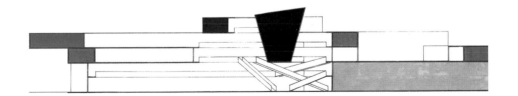

OPPOSITE, FROM ABOVE L TO R: *Horizontal sections of model – roof; fourth floor isolation cells; third floor cell-block; second floor cell-blocks with three patios; first floor containing offices and services with two patios; ground floor containing entrance, workshops, gym and offices, with one patio*, FROM ABOVE: *Sketch perspective of interior; sections*

De Grittenborgh Penitentiary

Hoogeveen, The Netherlands

OD 205

Situated on the outskirts of Hoogeveen, this 'H'-shaped complex is one of a series of prisons built at the end of the 1980s. The brief required a structure that would incorporate 252 cells, of which 12 were to be isolated in a top security unit. Enough space was also required for the usual correctional facilities such as work places, sport, recreation, visiting and services. A double security system was realised by means of a 5-metre high concrete wall and enclosed prison yards.

Symmetry plays an important role in the design; expressed in the floor plan and elevations. The building is divided into two nearly identical halves by a central corridor. All cells are accommodated in two long wings, partly in three levels, one above the other, and partly in two.

The living rooms and all other rooms for leisure activities are located in the transverse connections between the two wings. The central axis includes facilities for administrative staff and prison attendants. A small triangular-shaped building houses the entrance, reception and check-in areas, and the conference and executive rooms.

The plan and colour of this building echo the red, white and blue flag of The Netherlands. De Grittenborgh is constructed entirely of concrete, utilising a material able to satisfy high aesthetic standards despite its association with bad construction work in the past. The artistic effects of the wall exploit this skilfully, while double windows to each cell, painted dark blue and barred, provide further aesthetic and spatial resonances.

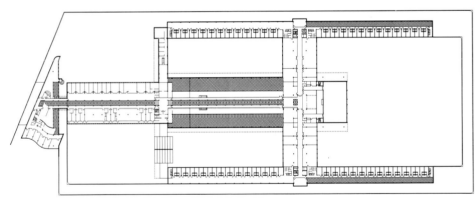

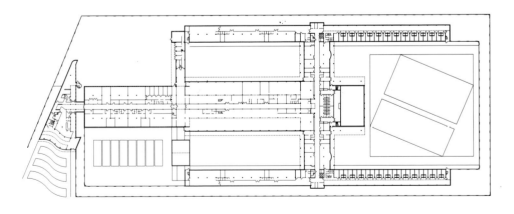

First floor plan; ground floor plan

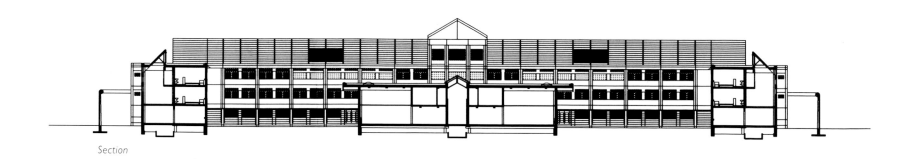

Section

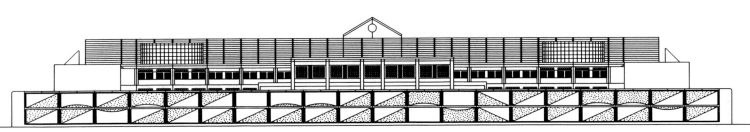

Section showing decorative wall treatment

De Schie Penitentiary

Rotterdam, The Netherlands

CAREL WEEBER / DE ARCHITECTEN CIE

Relatively isolated on an industrial site not far from the city centre, is De Schie Penitentiary on the Delfshavense Schie River. This complex, completed in 1988, is known as the 'golden sphinx'.

Of rectangular form, it comprises 200 × 80 metres. Two spacious courts are enclosed and overlooked by all cells. Together, the 252 cells take up only 15 per cent of the gross surface area; the rest is absorbed by offices, workshops, kitchens, recreation rooms and visiting rooms.

Consciously set away from the road is the entrance, discreetly interrupting the continuum that is the wall. Almost invisible, it turns away from the city; the shorter side of the complex facing the street. The wall is 5 metres high; like a classical plinth it forms part of the building.

The glazed, ochre facades of the penitentiary's long sides complement the glass and grey metal of the Van Nelle tobacco factory opposite, which was designed by Brinkman and Van der Vlugt. Glass is exploited effectively for facades, sheds and windows and permits as much light as possible. Adequate solutions are provided by combined use of laminated glass.

The colours of the rendered stripes in the head elevations are ochre and blue. Windows and bars are green and the edges red. In the symmetrically ordered interior, colours recall Southern climates.

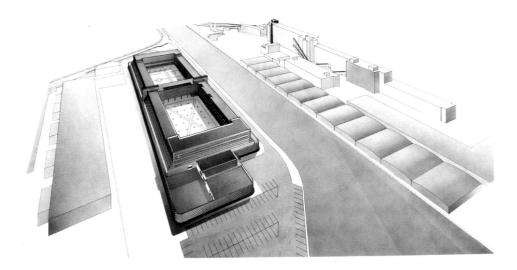

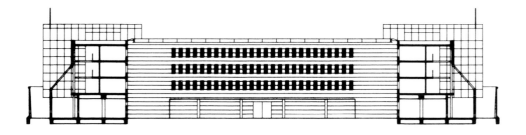

ABOVE: *Aerial perspective of site;* RIGHT: *Section. (Photography: Piet Rook.)*

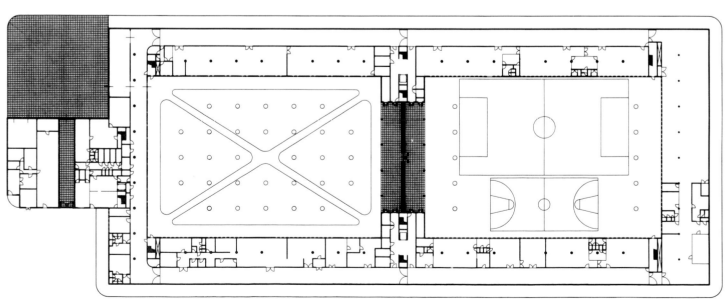

Ground floor plan

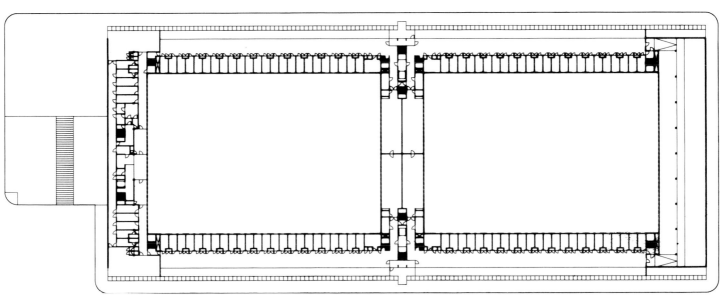

First floor plan

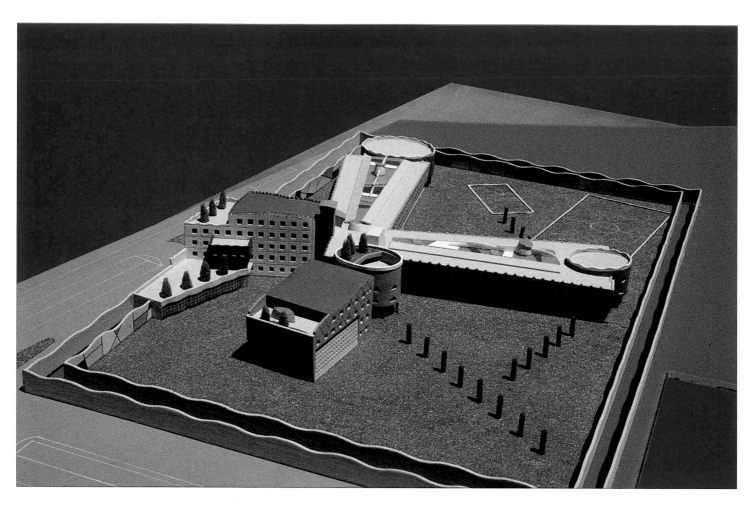

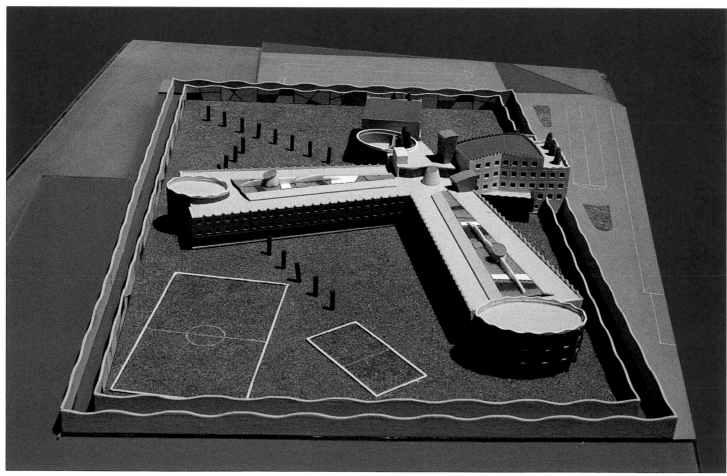

Penitentiary Design for Dordrecht
The Netherlands

TOMÁS TAVEIRA

The design for this penitentiary was the result of a limited competition organised by the public works ministry of the Dutch Government. The brief required careful consideration of the rules of freedom and movement limitation and visual control.

Taveira made note of the topography of Dordrecht and local building features and characteristics of the area. The resultant design attempts to create a prison that is a small town; a microcosm wherein 'plazas', streets, local entertainment and various meeting points engender a less stifling environment.

This is formed by a cross with unequal arms. The bulk of cellular accommodation is contained in two buildings which are developed in three storeys, including prisoner labour areas and technical facilities. The coloured and highly decorated wall in one building is inspired by the work of Mondrian and separates its two 24-cell wings, which are not parallel but open up, justifying the appearance of a new form at the end for the living leisure areas. Five isolation cells with patios (open space cages) are provided for.

The residential areas, which are positioned at right angles to each other, terminate in oval access towers. These are balanced beyond the crossing by smaller buildings; a high security oval tower, a rectangular gym, further accommodation and administration facilities.

Each building is formed and shaped in a highly individualistic way with imaginative use of colour. Aesthetic character is unabashed by the traditional associations and nature of the penitentiary. The project evokes the world of children's 'comic strips' with Dick Tracy as the hero.

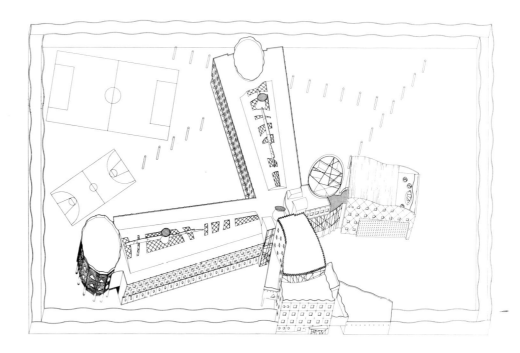

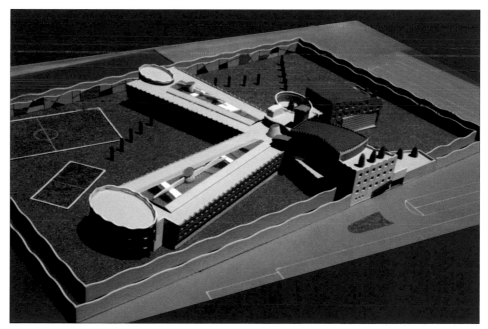

ABOVE: *Axonometric*

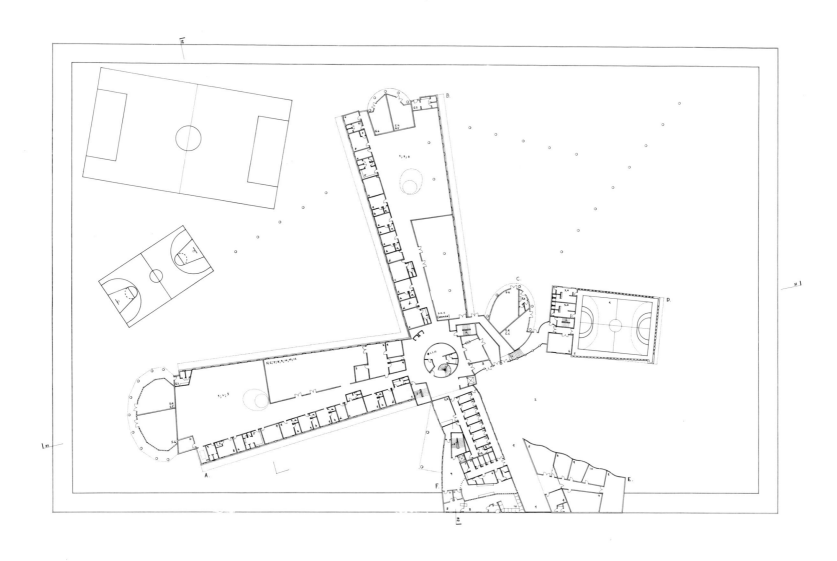

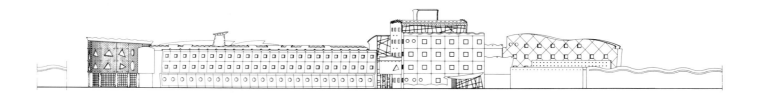

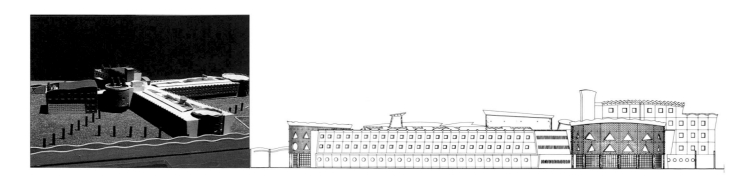

FROM ABOVE: *First floor plan; elevations*

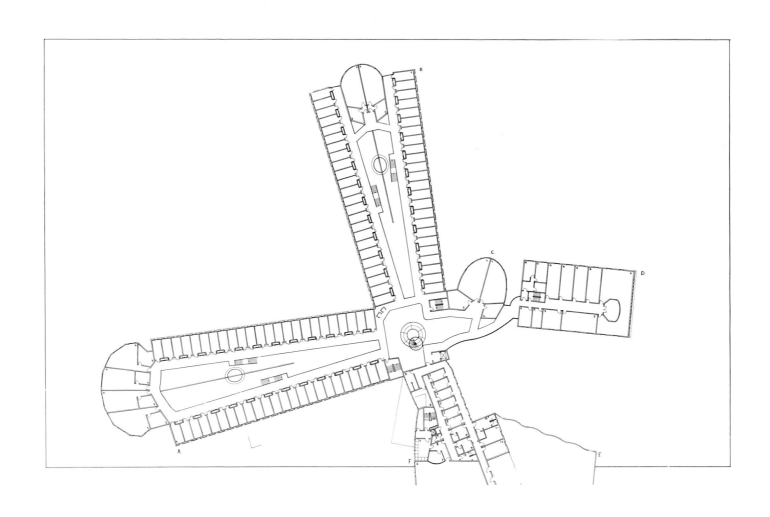

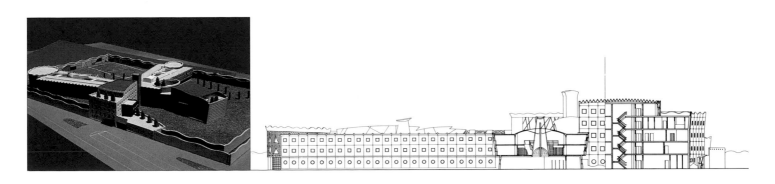

FROM ABOVE: *Third floor plan; sections*

Brians Penitentiary Centre
Barcelona, Spain

GOVERNMENT OF CATALONIA

To respond effectively to changing situations in the structuring of the prison population in Catalonia, the new penitentiary centres are conceived and designed in accordance with a flexible, modular approach.

The spatial and operational programme is based upon the following criteria: conception of buildings which meet the requirements of dignity, security and durability; creation of a setting which facilitates organisation of peaceful coexistence and the execution of many activities, to encourage re-education and reintegration with society; sufficient provision of space and facilities to ensure an adequate level for the services which the penitentiary administration provides for inmates; drawing up of a suitable spatial plan for the arrangement of the various residential units. This allows internal classification of inmates to be more efficient and ensures that a higher level of functional flexibility exists.

The aim is to create a setting that is conducive to personal development and positive change, where potential exists for action and intervention; both within the institution and with the community at large.

Brians Penitentiary was completed in 1992 to accommodate 1,100 male and female imates. It is situated near St Esteve Sesrovires, a small town outside Barcelona. The modular design of the complex seeks to invoke an urban environment by offering different spatial situations for occupational activities and exploiting fully the transitional aspects. Throughout the complex, retaining walls, unevenness, open horizons, distances and shadows help to create an environment with less spatial repetition to ward off monotony.

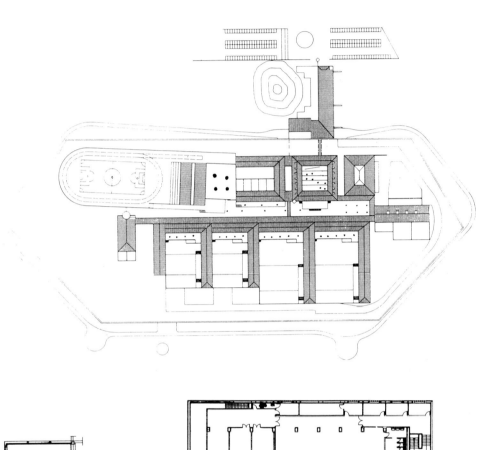

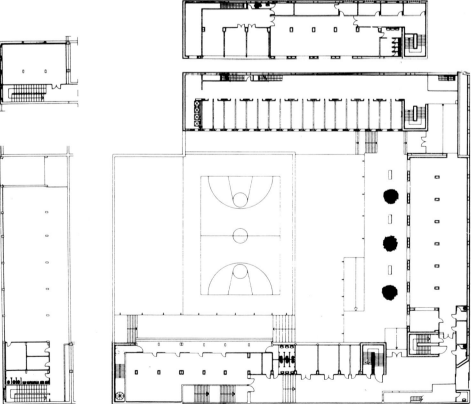

FROM ABOVE: *Plans of penitentiary layout and residential module*

Maison d'Arrêt d'Epinal
Les Vosges, France

GUY AUTRAN

This project places emphasis on the idea of 'the street', key in the co-ordination of various areas. Prisoners are able to move from one area to another within their confined space, as if in any normal community. This encourages a more positive interaction with their environment. The long atrium, which includes enclosed surveillance, makes use of glass and light effects, colour and furnishings which are not so institutional in appearance, in order to create a less imposing and harsh structure for new arrivals. This allows them to adapt more easily, and in a shorter time frame, to their carceral situation.

Cellular units, off 'the street', are provided with a large, multi-use area which is divided by walls of glass. Long arcades serve to create a more pleasant interior space. Autran rejected the rectangular cell arrangement in favour of a less oppressive space which was created by interesting geometrical effects to amplify and enliven the space; while taking care not to affect room surveillance for the guard.

This angular emphasis occurs throughout the prison to create a variety of interesting perspectives for the confined inmate. The visual impact of the prison is extended to the customary wall of enclosure, which uses colour and geometrical effects to reduce the height of the building itself.

This prison does not shy away from playing with space, light and colour, and makes use of simple, resistant and economical materials. It takes into consideration a key factor of the carceral process: preparing the inmate for reintegration

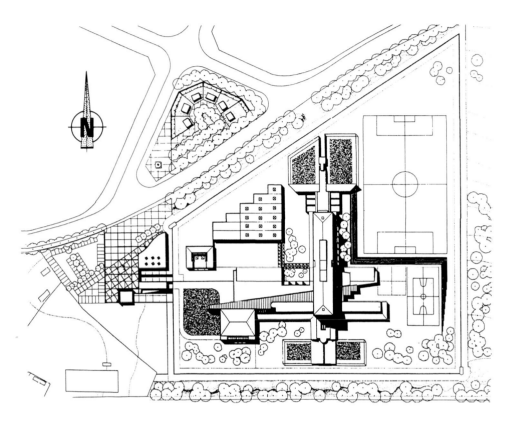

ABOVE: *Site plan*

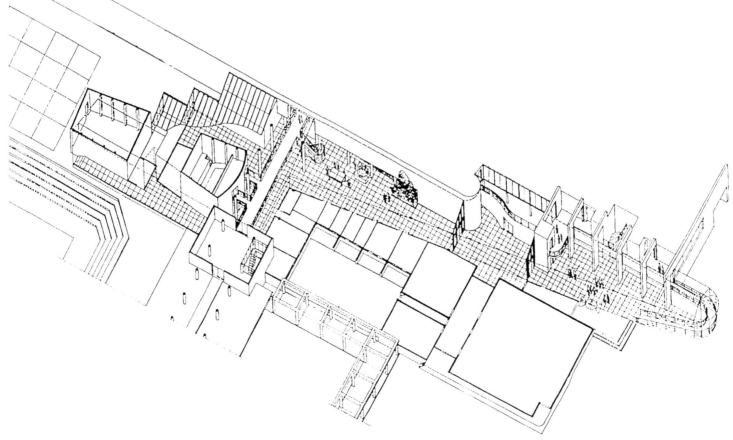

Axonometric showing 'the street'

Interior perspective

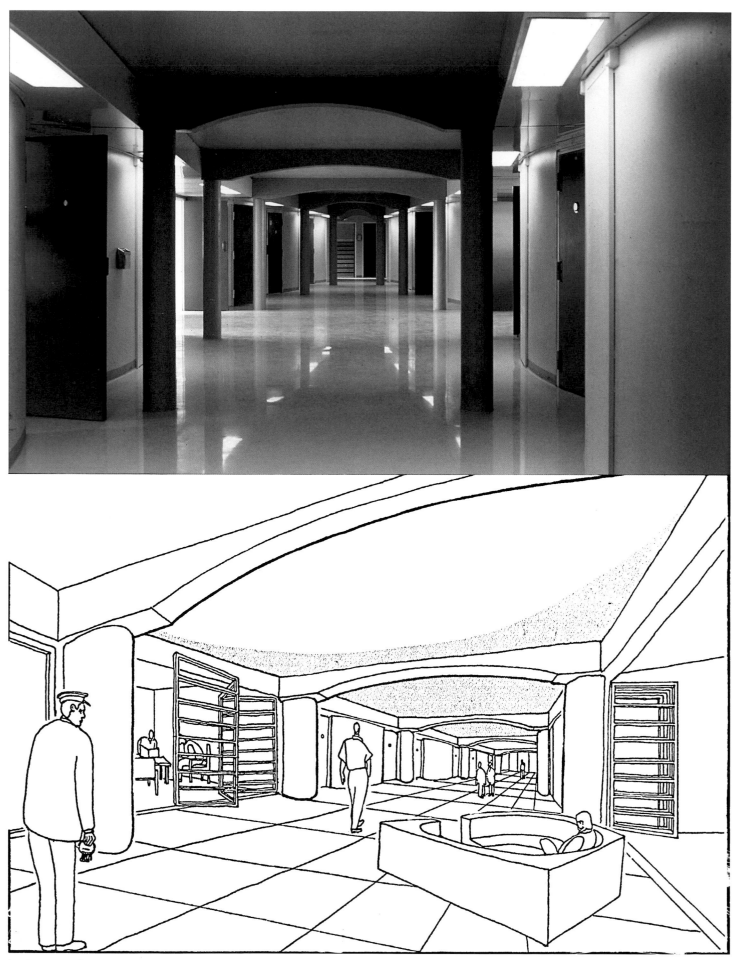

Interior perspective

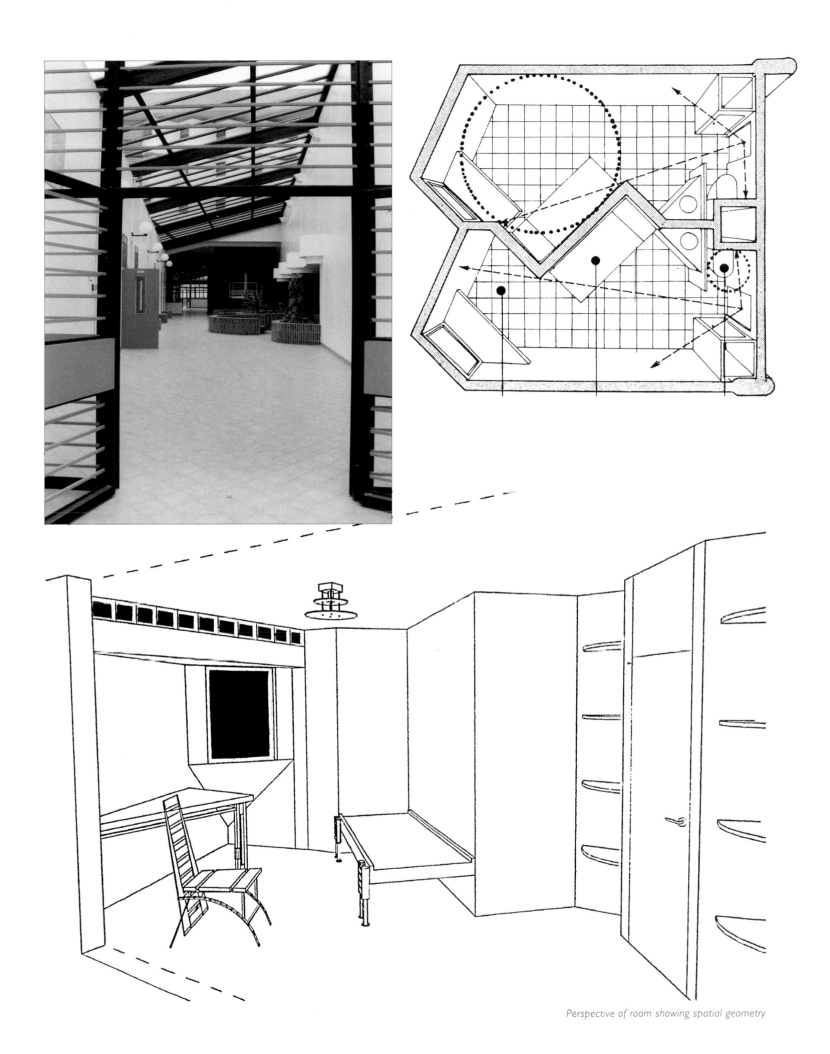

Perspective of room showing spatial geometry

Maison d'Arrêt de Brest

Brest, France

REMY BUTLER

This prison in Brest opened its doors in 1990 to accommodate 220 inmates, consisting of men, women and young offenders, for short term detention.

The severe austerity of the exposed concrete walls evokes harsh associations, yet is a significant contrast to the interior which is designed to encourage communication, rather than effect sensorial privation so often induced by the traditional penal model. Enclosed within the sculptural mass are the social and medical places, gymnasium, laboratories, general housing, courtyards, sportsground and cultural facilities. Administration, storage, semi-liberty area and parlours are located outside this area.

At Brest, the psychological quality of the inmates' life has been taken into consideration, initiating a spatially stimulating environment that is filled with light and colour wherein the confined inmates can move about with more freedom. Bright colours arc applied to surfaces throughout the building, for example in activity areas, service facilities, columns, doors and details; the cell interiors are of a lighter, softer tone that is accentuated by colour features.

This monumental building is positioned in a north-south direction which serves to exploit fully the qualities of light. Vast windows and surfaces in concrete-framed glass blocks allow sunlight to penetrate the building and enliven surfaces.

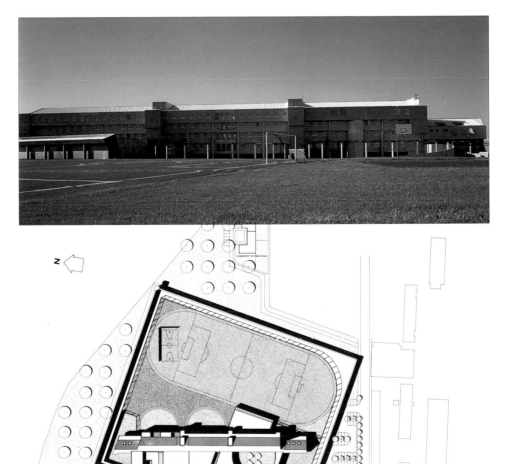

ABOVE: *Site plan. (Photography: Deidi Von Schaewen.)*

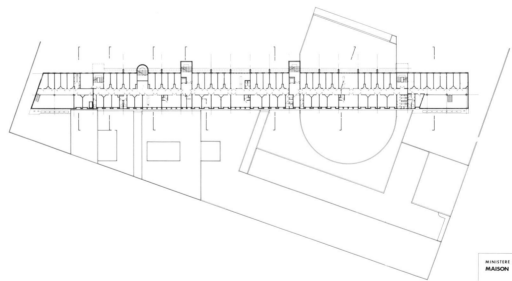

MINISTERE
MAISON

OPPOSITE: *Ground floor plan*; ABOVE: *Second floor plan*

References and Select Bibliography

Beccaria, C B, Crimes and Punishments, Livorno, 1764

Bowring, John, 'Panopticon; or, the Inspection House' (1791), Collected Works, Vol IV, London and Edinburgh, 1843

Buildings and Society: Essays on the Social Development of the Built Environment, edited by Anthony King, Routledge and Kegan Paul, London, 1980

Evans, Robin, The Fabrication of Virtue: English Prison Architecture, 1750-1840, Cambridge University Press, 1982

Foucault, Michel, Discipline and Punish: The Birth of the Prison (1975), Penguin Books, London 1991

Genet, Jean, The Thief's Journal (1949), Penguin Books, London 1967

Howard, John, The State of the Prisons in England and Wales, Warrington, 1777; third edition 1784
– An Account of the Principal Lazarettos, Warrington, 1789; second edition 1791

Ignatieff, Michael, A Just Measure of Pain: The Penitentiary in the Industrial Revolution, 1750-1850, Macmillan, London, 1978

Markus, Thomas A, Buildings and Power: Freedom and Control in the Origin of Modern Building Types, Routledge, London, 1993

Mayhew, H and Binny, J The Criminal Prisons of London and Scenes of Prison Life, Cass, London, 1862 (reprinted 1968, 1971)

Melossi, D and Pavarini, M, The Prison and the Factory: Origins of the Penitentiary System, Macmillan, London, 1981

Prison Architecture, UNSDRI (United Nations Social Defence Research Institute; now UNICRI), Rome, 1975

Rosenau, H, Social Purpose in Architecture, Paris and London Compared, 1760-1800, November Books, Studio Vista, London 1970

Semple, Janet, Bentham's Prison: A Study of the Panopticon Penitentiary, Clarendon Press, Oxford, 1993

Weisser, M R, Crime and Punishment in Early Modern Europe, Harvester Press, Brighton, 1979

Articles and other publications

Architecture for Justice. Exhibition reviews produced annually by AIA Press, 1735 New York Avenue, NW, Washington DC 20006

'Architecture for Punishment', Bauwelt, Vol 81, No 14, April 13, 1990, pp708-726

Building Types Study 705: 'Correctional Facilities in the United States', Architectural Record, Vol 181, No 5, May 1993, pp94-103

Dunbar, Ian, A Sense of Direction, Home Office Report, 1985

Fairweather, L, 'Modernising Strangeways', The Architects' Journal, 2 June 1993, pp29-42
– 'Prisons' (Woodhill, Milton Keynes). The Architects' Journal, 2 September, 1992, pp28-43
– 'Prisons: A New Generation', The Architects' Journal, 16 March 1989, pp26-31

First Report of Board of Directors of Prisons in Scotland, 1840, National Library of Scotland archives

Managing the Long Term Prison System, Report of the Home Office Control Review Committee, HMSO, London 1984

Markus, Thomas A, Order in Space and Society: Architectural Form and its Context in the Scottish Enlightenment, (ed and co-author) Mainstream, Edinburgh 1982
– 'Pattern of the Law', Architectural Review CXVI, pp251-6

'Maison d'Arret de Brest-Quimper', Arca, No 43, November 1990, pp8-17

National Institute of Corrections (NIC) publications:
– 'Proceedings of Second Annual Symposium of New Generation Jails, May 1987
– 'Proceedings of First Annual Symposium on Direct Supervision Jails', May 1 1986
– Larimer County Detention Center: A Study of Podular Direct Supervision, August 1987
– Pima County Detention Center: A Study of Podular Direct Supervision, January 1987
– 'Small Jail Design Guide: A Planning and Design Resource for Local Facilities of up to 50 Beds', March 1988

New Directions in Prison Design, Report of a Home Office Working Party on American New Generation Prisons, HMSO, London, 1985

'New Dutch Prisons', BOUW, Vol 44, No 20, October 6, 1989, pp15-20

'Prison Design and Construction', Construction, special issue, No 77, September 1990, pp41-92, London

Prison Design Briefing System (PDBS). Home Office Library Publications, London, 1988; updated 1989, 1990, 1991

'Prisons', Baumeister, Vol 90, No 7, July 1993, pp11-46

'Prisons', Deutsche Bauzeitung, Vol 126, No 5, May 1992, pp13-122

'Prisons: United States', Progressive Architecture, Vol 74, No 2, February 1993, pp51-57

'Reforming the Reformatory', Arche (AIA) Vol 82, No 2, February 1993

'Survey of Prisons in the Netherlands', Architect (The Hague), Vol 17, No 4, April 1986, pp60-71; No 5, May 1986, pp66-101; No 6, June 1986, pp56-71

White Paper: Prison Disturbances April 1990, Report of an enquiry by the Rt Hon Lord Justice Woolf, HMSO, London, 1984

White Paper: Custody Care and Justice, The Way Ahead for the Prison Service in England and Wales, HMSO, London 1991